EVOLVING

PUBLIC

CULTURE

EVOLVING PUBLIC CULTURE

SHAME AND WOUNDING AS PORTALS TO POWER, POTENCY, AND POTENTIAL

JOY IS THE BYPRODCUT OF LIVING YOUR UNIQUE SELF

• • •

From Conscious Evolution 1.0 to Conscious Evolution 2.0

One Mountain, Many Paths: Oral Essays
Volume Five

DR. MARC GAFNI AND
BARBARA MARX HUBBARD

Author: Marc Gafni and Barbara Marx Hubbard
Title: Evolving Public Culture
From Conscious Evolution 1.0 to Conscious Evolution 2.0

Identifiers: ISBN 979-8-88834-082-0 (electronic)
ISBN 979-8-88834-081-3 (paperback)

Edited by Timothy Paul Aryeh, Dorothea Betz, and Rachel Keune

World Philosophy and Religion Press, St. Johnsbury, VT
in conjunction with

IP Integral Publishers

https://worldphilosophyandreligion.org

JOIN THE REVOLUTION!

CONTENTS

CHAPTER 3 REDEFINING IDENTITY: RESPONDING TO THE TRANSGENDER QUESTION AND RAPE CULTURE WITH EVOLUTIONARY SPIRITUALITY

CHAPTER 4 AN EVOLUTIONARY CHURCH COLLECTIVE IS A SYMPHONY OF UNIQUE EXPRESSIONS OF LOVEINTELLIGENCE

EDITORIAL NOTE ABOUT AUTHORSHIP, EDITING, AND THE RADICAL CONTEXT FOR THIS SERIES

ORAL ESSAYS FROM THE ONE MOUNTAIN, MANY PATHS WEEKLY BROADCAST

This volume is part of the Oral Essays library, a series of lightly edited, compiled transcripts of oral teachings given by Dr. Marc Gafni and the late Barbara Marx Hubbard in their weekly online broadcast, *One Mountain, Many Paths,* which they co-founded in 2017. Originally called an "Evolutionary Church," *One Mountain, Many Paths* became a key venue for the articulation of an inspired and deeply grounded new Story of Value in response to the meta-crisis. Marc and Barbara—together with Zak Stein,[1] Kristina Kincaid, Ken Wilber, Sally Kempton, Lori Galperin, Aubrey Marcus and dozens of other thought-leaders over the years—began to articulate what they call a World Philosophy and World Religion[2] as a context for our diversity.

---

1 Zak, together with Ken Wilber, has been Marc's primary intellectual partner and an initiate lineage holder in CosmoErotic Humanism.

2 This project is grounded in four core organizational frameworks: 1) The Center for World Philosophy and Religion, co-founded by Marc Gafni, Zachary Stein, Sally Kempton, and Ken Wilber, and chaired over the years by John P. Mackey, Barbara Marx Hubbard, Aubrey Marcus, Gabrielle Anwar and Shareef Malnik, Carrie Kish and Adam Bellow, and Kathleen J. Brownback. 2) The Office for the Future, chaired by Stephanie Valcke and Ivan Bossyut. 3) The World Philosophy and Religion Press, founded and chaired by Aubrey Marcus, together with Marc Gafni and Zachary Stein. 4) The Foundation for Conscious Evolution, founded by Barbara Marx Hubbard and currently chaired by Peter Fiekowsky. For a complete list of key leadership, see the Office for the Future website, www.officeforthefuture.com.

Until Barbara's passing in 2019, she and Marc transmitted teachings together as evolutionary partners and "whole mates," weaving together insights and transmissions from their decades of practice, study, teaching, and activism into a synergy of wisdom, a grounded vision for future policy across all sectors of society.

Much of the *dharma* material below comes directly from Marc, so it was originally all in quotation marks—but that looked a little odd. So per his suggestion we removed them, and the reader should consider the paragraphs on the next several pages as one extended quote from him. We are joyfully grateful to Marc for the clarity of his *dharma*, the elegance and "second simplicity" of this language, and the mad, Outrageous Love with which he transmits his teachings.

Barbara and Marc called the mission of *One Mountain* "a Planetary Awakening in Evolutionary Love Through Unique Self Symphonies." We are an evolutionary community with a deeply grounded, radically alive, and "post-tragic" revolutionary spirit. We are activating a new humanity and awakening as a new species: *Homo amor*, the fulfillment of *Homo sapiens*.

One Mountain is committed to articulating a Story of Value that can become the ground for the new society that must be birthed in response to the meta-crisis. We recognize that we are living at a pivotal moment in history. In this "time between stories," the great moral imperative is to tell the new Story of Value. It is ours to do, personally and collectively, with great trembling and ecstatic joy.

FROM DOGMA TO *DHARMA*: ETERNAL AND EVOLVING FIRST PRINCIPLES AND FIRST VALUES

The teachings are grounded in decades of deep study across many wisdom traditions. Over the years, week by week, these teachings were incrementally developed within the framework of the *One Mountain, Many Paths* broadcast. We often refer to these teachings as *dharma*.

This word was originally used in lineage traditions to refer to something like universal law. This is a crucial realization: just as there is universal law in mathematical value, there is also a sense of universal law in ethics and value.

Historically, *dharma* often devolved into unchanging dogma. Evolution was ignored, and the natural process of *dharma* evolution became disconnected from its deep, eternal context. The weakness of the word *dharma* is that too often it did not include the evolving insights of the sciences, it confused local cultural truths with universal truths, and it used words like "eternal," as in "eternal Tao," as opposed to words like "evolution."

Eternal came to mean unchanging, and that kind of thinking often led to overly ethnocentric readings of *dharma*. Local systems would claim their religious and cultural insights as immutable, which stood in the way of the emergence of a genuine world Story of Value that is real, inherent to Cosmos, and backed by the Universe—even as it is also always evolving.

Or, as we often say, "eternal value is evolving value. The eternal Tao is the evolving Tao."

We have shown that, emergent from profound insights in the "interior sciences," eternal does not mean unchanging in time; it means what we call the deeper Field of ErosValue that is beneath culture, geography, and history, which lives beneath all individual and collective values, and beneath time and space itself.

As such, we have gradually transitioned from the term *dharma* to the term *Value*, in the sense of the Field of Value that lives beneath all values. This Field of Value discloses as First Principles and First Values embedded in a Story of Value.

Indeed, as the interior sciences knew and the exterior sciences imply, Reality arises in a Field of ErosValue in which an entire set of mathematical, musical, molecular, moral, and mystical values are the very ground of all being. That Field of Value is eternal—the true ground of the Good, True and Beautiful—even as it is evolving.

But of course, it is equally critical not just to talk about evolving value, but to ground the evolving value in its true nature, the eternal Field of First Principles and First Values, always reaching for ever-more life, ever-more love, ever-more care, ever-more depth, ever-more uniqueness, ever-more intimate communion, and ever-more transformation.

As such, when we refer to the word *dharma*, which still appears in these texts together with the word value, we refer to an evolving *dharma* grounded in an *eternal and evolving* Field of Value. Indeed, eternity and evolution are two faces of the whole, opposites joined at the hip, that characterize the nature of our Cosmos in virtually all of its expressions.

It's in these terms that we ground a robust world philosophy that integrates the validated, leading-edge insights of premodern traditional wisdom, modern wisdom, and more recent postmodern insights, weaving them together into a new whole greater than the sum of its parts.

This new whole is a shared Story of Value rooted in First Principles and First Values that are both eternal and evolving.

These First Principles and First Values of Cosmos are woven together into a new Story of Value as a context for our diversity, a new Universe Story. This new Story gives us the best possible responses we have to the mystery, and to the great questions:

- Who am I? Who are we?
- Where am I? Where are we?
- What should I do? What should we do?

It is only through such a shared Universe Story—a narrative of identity and ethos as a context for our blessed diversity—that we can realize how what unites is so much greater than what divides us.

Only a new Story of Value will allow us to both respond to the meta-crisis and participate together in birthing the most true, good, and beautiful world that we already know is possible.

THIS ORAL ESSAYS SERIES IS AN ENTRYWAY TO THE GREAT LIBRARY OF COSMOEROTIC HUMANISM

This Oral Essays series is part of the overarching project of the Great Library at the Center for World Philosophy and Religion, led by Dr. Marc Gafni, together with Dr. Zak Stein. The aim of the Great Library project is to articulate a robust and comprehensive new Story of Value, CosmoErotic Humanism, in the form of dozens of well-researched and extensively footnoted academic works.

Our vision is to provide the philosophical framework that will be vital for navigating humanity through this time of immense crisis and transformation.

To begin your journey into CosmoErotic Humanism, we tenderly refer you to the book *First Principles and First Values*, co-authored by Marc Gafni, Zak Stein, and Ken Wilber, under the name David J. Temple. David J. Temple is a pseudonym created for enabling ongoing collaborative authorship at the Center for World Philosophy and Religion. The two primary authors behind David J. Temple are Marc Gafni and Zak Stein, and for different projects, specific writers will be named as part of the collaboration, such as Ken Wilber and others.

Three other volumes complete this introduction: *A Return to Eros*, by Marc Gafni and Kristina Kincaid; *Your Unique Self*, by Marc Gafni; and *Education in a Time between Worlds*, by Zak Stein.

We hope that the Oral Essays in this volume, with their informal style of transmission, will serve as an allurement and entryway for you into the more formal books of the Great Library that provide the robust intellectual underpinnings of the new Story of Value.

A NOTE ABOUT THE EDITORS

This Oral Essays collection has been edited by students of the new Story of CosmoErotic Humanism. Each of us has actively participated in *One Mountain, Many Paths*, and most of us have been in deep "Holy of Holies" study with Dr. Marc Gafni for many years.

We have been privileged to find ourselves well-versed in the teachings, and even emerging as lineage-holders of CosmoErotic Humanism.[3]

We view this editing project as a privilege and a deep practice of study and clarification. We experience ourselves as a *mystical editing society*, frequently meeting and conversing together about the content—the depth of knowledge and wisdom offered here—as well as the technical intricacies involved with publishing a beautiful and coherent series of books. In so doing, we function as a "Unique Self Symphony," which itself is a Dharmic

---

3 CosmoErotic Humanism is a world philosophical movement aimed at reconstructing the collapse of value at the core of global culture. Much like Romanticism or Existentialism, CosmoErotic Humanism is not merely a theory but a movement that changes the very mood of Reality. It is an invitation to participate in evolving the source code of consciousness and culture towards a cosmocentric *ethos* for a planetary civilization.

The term CosmoErotic Humanism, initially coined by Dr. Gafni and colleagues, points to a complex, multi-faceted, layered, and nuanced evolutionary set of insights that has evolved over decades of intensive research, teaching, and spiritual practice from deep within a wide range of wisdom traditions (including the Wisdom of Solomon lineage tradition, Bodhisattva Buddhism, and Kashmir Shaivism), as well as multiple disciplines including complexity theory, chaos theory, emergence theory, molecular biology, and the more classical disciplines of the humanities.

The seeds of CosmoErotic Humanism were planted with Dr. Marc Gafni's work on a two-volume, 1,000-page opus called *Radical Kabbalah* (Integral Publishers, 2012). This scholarly work, sourced from deep study within the esoteric lineage texts of the Wisdom of Solomon, points to a non-dual, or acosmic, realization which—unlike the prevailing conceptualization of non-duality—does not efface the human being; rather, it is highly humanistic in its nature. The next step in the evolution of CosmoErotic Humanism was the insight that all of Reality is evolving Eros, which lives in, as, and through the human being.

A failure of Eros leads inexorably to the creation of narratives of "pseudo-eros." CosmoErotic Humanism is a response to the modern mental and social breakdown sourced in the proliferation of multiple forms of pseudo-eros and its broken narratives, such as rivalrous conflict governed by win/lose metrics and the dogmatic denial of intrinsic value in Cosmos, which together generate our current "global intimacy disorder."

term that connotes an omni-considerate collaboration between realized Unique Selves synergizing our unique gifts into a new emergence greater than the sum of the parts. Even as we worked diligently to standardize our editing styles, meeting on a weekly basis to debate the nuances of phrasing, we also operated from within a deep appreciation of the unique style that each editor brought to his or her work. As such, the reader might notice some variation in editing style among the books.

Please note that Dr. Marc Gafni has not reviewed these edited Oral Essays, as he is deeply engaged in writing the formal books of the Great Library. But he has been generous in responding to questions and providing overall guidance in the project. Overall, as Marc's students and students of the *dharma*, we have made it a key project at the Center to publish these pieces of work relatively independently.

OUR UNIQUE ORAL-ESSAY EDITING STYLE PRESERVES THE ENERGY OF THE ORIGINAL TRANSMISSION

Dr. Marc Gafni is a uniquely gifted teacher whose oral transmission is imbued with a quality that has proven transformative for his students. Many of us feel mystically transformed by both the content and the underlying energy of the transmission style. Therefore, as we like to say, *trust the magic ways the dharma comes through your unique understanding!*

As Marc's empowered students, colleagues, and beloved friends, we have a deep knowing that these teachings are vital for the survival and thriving of humanity as we know it, and we recognize the importance of publishing his teachings in a written format that will be accessible by future generations. At the same time, we sought to preserve the Eros of the original oral transmission with all of its nuance, power, and depth. Our intention in the editing process, to the greatest extent possible, has been to keep these spoken artifacts intact in order to maintain the flow of the original transmission. We have therefore chosen not to engage in intensive formal editing, as we found that doing so resulted in the loss of the energetic transmission that is so key to fully receiving the *dharma*.

After experimenting with many ways to present these texts, we developed a specific way of laying out the text on the page. Marc, in collaboration with Zak Stein and Russian intellectual/artist Elena Maslova-Levin—and ultimately all of the editors, through many conversations—developed a unique, artistic presentation of the text, using bolding, italics, bullet points, and other stylistic features which together serve to accentuate the immediacy of the oral transmission.

As part of this editing style, intended to preserve the integrity of the original transmission, we have refrained from removing the frequent recapitulations of key themes. We found that each recapitulation contributes something vital to the rhythm and music beneath the words, like the beating drum of our hearts. These recapitulations not only review previous material but also add important new emphases, perspectives, and elements of the new Story of Value. We ask for your patience as a reader to trust the rhythm of these texts, and we trust you as a reader to have the depth and steadiness to find your way through.

KEY COMPONENTS: LINK TO THE ORIGINAL BROADCAST, EVOLUTIONARY LOVE CODES AND PRAYER

To supplement the written word, each episode includes a QR code linking to the original broadcast on YouTube, as well as occasional links to featured songs and video clips.

Each episode also centers around an "Evolutionary Love Code," formulated by Marc. These codes are part of the ongoing articulation and distillation of the *dharma* as it unfolds and emerges, week by week, over the course of many years, through the mystical process we call Outrageous Love or Evolutionary Love.

Another core component of the *One Mountain, Many Paths* episodes is what Marc and Barbara called "Evolutionary Prayer." Prayer is experienced in *One Mountain* not in the old fundamentalist sense of a "cosmic vending-machine god" who is alienated from Cosmos. Marc refers to this as the "god you do not and should not believe in"—and he often adds, "the god you don't believe in does not exist."

GOD IS THE INFINITE INTIMATE

In fact, in the *dharma* of CosmoErotic Humanism, a new name for God has emerged: the "Infinite Intimate," who appears in first-, second-, and third-person expressions. Marc first shared this name as he heard it whispered in 2023, although earlier intimations and formulations of the name appeared as early as 2010.

In first person, God is infinitely alive and as intimate as our own first-person experience.

In second person, God is the infinitely intimate Personhood of Cosmos that knows our name and holds us—the God about whom we say, *whenever we fall, we fall into Her hands.* This is the God who is our Beloved, Father, Mother, Lover, and Evolutionary Partner.

Finally, in third person, God inheres in all of the First Principles and First Values of Cosmos, and in the laws of science (both interior and exterior) that govern manifest Reality.

Therefore, we have a realization of God as not only the Infinity of Power but also the Infinity of Intimacy.

In *One Mountain, Many Paths*, we are reclaiming prayer at a higher level of consciousness. And we are reclaiming prayer as deep, alive, loving, and intimate conversations with God as the Infinite Intimate who knows our name.

REFLECTING ON THE CO-CREATION BETWEEN DR. MARC GAFNI AND BARBARA MARX HUBBARD

Barbara and Marc met five years before Barbara passed. As Barbara said so often, "before I met Marc, I was sure that I was done." Barbara had taught so beautifully for decades, focusing particularly on a powerful articulation of "conscious evolution."

Indeed, it would not be inaccurate to say that Barbara was the greatest storyteller of conscious evolution of her time.

Conscious evolution was also a premise in Marc's thinking, but drawn from an entirely different set of sources and experiences. Barbara drew from the classical sources of evolutionary spirituality, such as Teilhard de Chardin, Buckminster Fuller, and many others. Indeed, she was closely associated with Fuller, and was perhaps de Chardin's most ardent intellectual devotee.

Marc drew a somewhat different vision of conscious evolution from the interior sciences of the great wisdom traditions, with a primary emphasis on what he refers to as the "Solomon lineages," merged together with careful readings of the leading edges of the sciences. In the old version of conscious evolution, the movement from unconscious to conscious was a movement of evolution by chance to evolution by choice.

Together Marc and Barbara evolved the old version of Conscious Evolution, pointing out that evolution itself was always in some sense conscious, but as Marc formulated it, the awakening to conscious evolution refers to the awakening of evolution as human consciousness, coupled with the human realization of being conscious evolution in person, and the human capacity to locate oneself within the context of the larger evolutionary story.

Marc focused his attention on an entirely different dimension of Reality, which he and his colleagues began to call CosmoErotic Humanism. The Intimate Universe, Homo amor, Unique Self and Unique Self Symphonies,

God as the Infinity of Intimacy, Eros and the CosmoErotic Universe, distinctions like Role Mate, Soul Mate and Whole Mate, the Four Selves, Evolutionary Love, Outrageous Love, Evolution: the Love Story of the Universe, First Principles and First Values, Evolving Perennialism, the Evolution of Love, and many more are terms articulated by Gafni and shared with Barbara in their conversation, study, and creative engagement.

Some terms they coined together, for example "a Planetary Awakening in Love through Unique Self Symphonies," where Gafni described Unique Self Symphonies, and Barbara aligned her vision of a planetary Pentecost to Marc's vision of Unique Self Symphonies.

Other key terms were unique and articulated by Barbara, for example: conscious evolution, teleros, telerotic, from joining genes to joining genius, regenopause, vocational arousal, birthing of humanity, synergy engine, and of course her work around what she called the Wheel of Co-creation. Ultimately, Marc and Barbara attempted to synergize their work in what they called the Wheel of Co-creation 2.0. Barbara and Marc experienced themselves as merging their respective *dharma* into what they began to refer to as Conscious Evolution 2.0, or later, CosmoErotic Humanism.

The first 129 episodes of One Mountain, Many Paths took place in the last period of Barbara's life and reflect the depth and texture of the stunning evolutionary whole-mate meeting between her and Marc. As Barbara was deep in study with Marc, a lot of what she shared in Evolutionary Church was the *dharma* of their deep study and collaboration.

Although sometimes it may be clear who is speaking, we generally publish these early episodes in what we are calling "one voice." The first 129 episodes, with Marc and Barbara together, have been grouped chronologically. Episodes 130 to 400 and onwards, which were transmitted by Marc, have been grouped by topic.

THE INVITATION

We invite you to find your way into this revolution. Each one of our Unique Selves and unique gifts are desperately needed as we co-create this new Story of Value together, as part of the covenant between generations, for the sake of the whole.

Let's *play a larger game* and evolve the very source code of consciousness and culture together.

With mad love,

The Editors

LOVE OR DIE

LOCATING OURSELVES: ARTICULATING THE ESSENTIAL CONTEXT FOR THE ONE MOUNTAIN, MANY PATHS ORAL ESSAYS

SETTING OUR INTENTION

Intention setting is everything.

We're here—as da Vinci was with his cohort in the Renaissance—**to play a larger game, to participate in the evolution of love, which is to tell the new Story of Value rooted in First Principles and First Values.**

- Our intention is to recognize the critical historical juncture in which we find ourselves.
- Our intention is to take our seat at the table of history and to say, *we take responsibility for this.*
- Our intention is to participate as revolutionaries for the sake of the whole.

What we're here to do is revolution; revolution for the sake of the evolution of love.

It's a revolution for the sake of the trillions of unborn lives that will not manifest:

- The unborn loves
- The unborn creativity
- The unborn goodness
- The unborn truth
- The unborn beauty

All of it looks to us.

Not because we're engaged in grandiosity. Not at all!

- We're trembling before She.
- We're trembling with joy at the privilege.
- We're trembling with joy at the responsibility.
- We're trembling with joy at the Possibility of Possibility.
- We have to enact a new Story in this moment of time. Because it is only a new Story that can change the vector of history.

The most revolutionary act that we can do—the greatest moral imperative of this time—**is to articulate a new Story at this time between worlds and this time between stories.**

Story is not made up, as postmodernity suggests. **We all live in inescapable frameworks; our framework is the story we live in.** Right now, Reality lives according to win/lose metrics, a story that is generating existential risk. **We need to change that story.**

When we change that story, when we tell a new Story—not a made-up story, but a new Story of Value, rooted in First Principles and First Values—**then it all changes.**

We need to participate in the evolution of the source code of consciousness and culture, which is the evolution of love.

It's the most important, exciting, evolutionary, revolutionary act that we can do to alleviate suffering: to be lovers.

Like Rumi, the great poet of Sufism, we have to be "mad lovers," because it's the only sanity.

To be mad lovers is to see around the corner, to not be so obsessed with the details of the contractions of my life.

Let me see bigger.

Let me take complete care of myself in every possible way, let me completely attend to those in my circle of intimacy and influence, and then—*let me expand my circle.*

That's what we're here for.

- Our intention is to participate in the *LoveForce*, the *LoveIntelligence*, the *LoveBeauty*, the *LoveDesire* that literally animates Cosmos all the way up and all the way down.
- Our intention is to participate in the evolution of love.

[In the next few pages we will cover some key concepts which are essential to locating ourselves and setting the context for all the One Mountain, Many Paths Oral Essays. —Eds.]

OVERVIEW: EROS IS NO LONGER A LUXURY—IT'S LOVE OR DIE

Eros is life.

The failure of Eros destroys life.

Our lack of Eros is poised to destroy the world.

All civilizations have fallen because the stories that they lived in were, in some sense, stories based on rivalrous conflict governed by win/lose metrics. Every civilization was weakened by interior polarization caused by the lack of a shared Story of Value.

We now have a global civilization, but we haven't created a shared Story of Value.

We haven't solved the generator functions that caused all civilizations to fall. Our global civilization has exponential technologies and extraction models depleting the Earth of resources that took billions of years to create, which is going to lead to a civilizational collapse.

Existential risk is risk to our very existence.

The choice is clear: love or die.

It's that simple.

Eros is no longer a luxury. It is an absolute necessity for the survival of the individual and the planet.

In the last half a century, modern psychology has documented an age-old truth: a fully nourished baby who is not held in loving arms will die.

So too, our world, both personal and global—even with all the resources of intelligence and technology at our disposal—will die without being held in love, in the embrace of Eros.

We must embrace a personal path of love and a global politics of love.

Not ordinary love. Not love which is "mere human sentiment," but Eros, or what we sometimes call Outrageous Love, which is the heart of existence itself.

We live in a world of outrageous pain.

The only response is Outrageous Love.

WHAT IS EROS?

Eros is the experience of radical aliveness, moving towards, seeking, desiring ever-deeper contact and ever-greater wholeness.[4] Eros is the core fabric of Reality's being and the motivational architecture of Reality's becoming.

Eros is what animates the evolutionary impulse itself, from the very inception of Cosmos all the way to our very selves, who awaken to the realization that the evolutionary impulse throbs uniquely in each of us.

The realization of human awakening and transformation that lies at the core of the interior sciences is the invitation—or even the urgent and desperate demand—of a madly loving Cosmos animated by infinities of power and infinities of intimacy.

The demand—the desperate invitation, the plea, the tender and fierce command of Cosmos that lives inside every human being—is to awaken: to awaken to our true nature as unique incarnations of Eros and Ethos that are needed and desperately desired by All-That-Is. Said slightly differently: Reality is Eros. Or: God is Eros.

The failure of Eros destroys life. The collapse of Eros is always the hidden (or not so hidden) root cause for the collapse of ethics.

This is true both personally and collectively. We live in a moment of a worldwide and personal collapse of Eros. Our lack of Eros is poised to destroy

---

4 We define Eros through what we refer to as the Eros equation (one of a series of what we call interior science equations):

> Eros = Radical Aliveness x Desiring (Growing + Seeking) x Deeper Contact
> x Greater Wholeness x Self Actualization/Self Transcendence (Creation
> [Destruction])

There are good reasons for the formal language of the interior science equations in these writings, and the reader is invited to explore them on their own, in particular, in our work, David J. Temple, *First Principles and First Values: Forty-Two Propositions on CosmoErotic Humanism, the Meta-Crisis, and the World to Come* (World Philosophy and Religion, 2024).

the world. Humanity is currently experiencing what has come to be known as existential risk, a risk to our very existence, or what I will refer to as the Second Shock of Existence.

EXISTENTIAL RISK: THE SECOND SHOCK OF EXISTENCE

The first shock of existence is the death of the human being—the realization that we will die, which dawns in human consciousness at the beginning of history. We are not talking about the biological fact of death but the *existential* realization of death. Although the interior sciences disclose that death is a portal between two days (there is vast empirical,[5] philosophical,[6] and anthro-ontological evidence[7] for the continuity of consciousness[8]), death is also, in our own direct surface experience, a stark end. And that is obviously not a bug but a feature in the system.

---

5 We refer to evidence gathered by the most serious of researchers, beginning with Henry and Edith Sedgwick at Cambridge University and William James at Harvard University, and continuing in highly rigorous form for the last 150 years, as recapitulated by Whiteheadian scholar David Ray Griffin in multiple volumes. See also, for example, Dean Radin, *Real Magic: Unlocking Your Natural Psychic Abilities to Create Everyday Miracles* (Potter/TenSpeed/Harmony, 2018), *The Conscious Universe: The Scientific Truth of Psychic Phenomena* (HarperCollins, 2010), and other books. Or see the earlier classic by Frederic William Henry Myers, *Human Personality and Its Survival of Bodily Death* (Longmans, Green, 1907).

6 This requires a cogent analysis of materialism and dualism, and the introduction of the far more cogent third possibility, which we have called "pan-interiority."

7 We discuss Anthro-Ontology in some depth in *First Principles and First Values*, and see also the fuller conversation in David J. Temple, *First Principles and First Values: Towards an Evolving Perennialism: Introducing the Anthro-Ontological Method*—both published by World Philosophy and Religion Press, in conjunction with Integral Publishers. For now, we will simply define it as an "innate and clear interior gnosis directly available to the human being."

8 See Dr. Marc Gafni and Dr. Zachary Stein's essay in preparation, "Beyond Death: Anthro-Ontology, Philosophy, and Empiricism." This essay is slated to appear in the book *Towards a World Religion: Homo Amor Essays.* The essay is also the ground for a larger book by the same authors, *Twelve Portals to Life Beyond Death: Responding to the Second Shock of Existence,* in which we discuss three forms of material: the empirical, the philosophical, and the anthro-ontological, and show how each form discredits the notion of death as the end.

Our first-person experience is that death ends this life. It is not the *totality* of our experience if we go deeper inside, but it is obviously intended to be the central, potent, and painful dimension of every human life. Indeed, as Ernest Becker potently reminded us, the denial of death is at our peril.

All the stories and all the plotlines and all the threads of living end at that moment. Whatever happens beyond, we have an actual experience of ending. **Paradoxically, that ending, the experience of the finality of mortality, is what presses us into life.** From the implicit demand of the first shock of existence, human beings were activated and pressed into creative emergence, and what emerged was all of human culture, both interior and exterior.

The second shock of existence is the realization of the potential death of all humanity. After all the stages of human history—matter, life, and mind in all of their stages of evolutionary unfolding—we have come to this place in the evolution of humanity, in which the gap between our exponentially expanding exterior technologies and our stalled (or even regressing) interior technologies of value has created dire catastrophic and existential risks.

This gap generates extraction models and exponential growth curves, rivalrous conflicts based on win/lose metrics, tragedies of the commons, and multipolar traps, in which everyone has to keep producing to the *n*th degree, including weaponized exponential threats to our very existence because we are afraid that the other parties are going to do it and not be transparent—hide it from us and then dominate us.

GENERATOR FUNCTIONS FOR EXISTENTIAL RISK

Let's outline clearly the main *generator functions for existential risk.*

Rivalrous conflicts governed by zero-sum, win/lose metrics. Rivalrous conflicts generate extraction models at the core of the economic system and exponential growth curves. Both of these drive and are driven by a contrived system of artificially manufactured desires and needs, delivered into culture by ever more precise forms of micro-targeting to individuals and groups through the ever more immersive environment of the internet.

Next, rivalrous conflicts and exponential growth curves animated by win/lose metrics generate **complicated, fragile world systems** highly vulnerable to myriad forms of collapse. Fragile local systems are made exponentially more fragile on a global level by our inability to meet global challenges with social, legal, political, economic, and ethical infrastructures that remain largely local.

All of this is a direct result of the failure to develop more adequate interior technologies that would be sufficiently compelling to displace "rivalrous conflict governed by win/lose metrics" as the motivational architecture for the human life world.

This failure has led to the conditions that will cause the implosion of systems that are already and quite literally on the brink of collapsing themselves. That's what we mean by the *second shock of existence*.

To recapitulate: the second shock of existence is not the death of the human being, but the potential death of humanity.

It is the *Death Star* moment of our species.

THE DECONSTRUCTION OF INTRINSIC VALUE

We stand in this moment poised between utopia and dystopia, at a time between worlds and a time between stories. We need a new Story of Value, eternal yet evolving, rooted in First Principles and First Values, which would become a universal grammar of value and a context for our diversity.

This is exactly what the Renaissance was. It was a time between worlds and a time between stories. In the Renaissance, we had recently been challenged by the Black Death, a pandemic that swept across Europe. The

Black Death destroyed between a third to half of Europe and a huge part of Asia. People died horrifically, brutally, in the streets. They had no idea how to meet this challenge, and so, in response to the Black Death, da Vinci and Ficino and their cohorts understood that they had to tell a new Story of Value.

That story was the story of modernity. Did they get it right?

- They got part of it right, which birthed, to use Jürgen Habermas' phrase, "the dignities of modernity," such as new ways of gathering information and universal human rights.
- But they also deconstructed the source of Value. They lost the basis for the Good, the True, and the Beautiful.

The basis used to be divine revelation: *God told us.* But this claim was owned by religion, and every religion began to overreach and over-claim. The revelation was thus often mediated through cultural categories and wasn't fully accurate.

Modernity threw out revelation, but was unable to establish a new basis for value.

Value was just assumed to be real. As it says in the founding document of the American Revolution: *We hold these truths to be self-evident*—that is, *we don't really have a basis for value; we just take it as a given.*

In other words, modernity took out a loan of social capital from the traditional world. The source of value was never worked out.

And then, gradually, value began to collapse.

- The Universe Story began to collapse.
- The belief that the Good, the True, and the Beautiful are real began to collapse.
- The belief that Love is real began to collapse.

As Bertrand Russell is reported to have said, "I cannot see how to refute the arguments for the subjectivity of ethical values, but I find myself incapable of believing that all that is wrong with wanton cruelty is that I do not like it."

What do you do if you grew up in a world in which value is not real? A world without a source of value, without a Universe Story, without a story of human identity, without a story of desire, without a narrative of power?

In the words of W.B. Yeats, *the center does not hold.*

- You have a collapse at the very center of society, because you no longer have Eros.
- You no longer have a Reality in which value is real, and so you have this lingering sense of emptiness.
- You have a complete collapse at the very center.
- We become *the hollow men and the stuffed men*, gesture without form.

And that's the source of our current existential risk.

THE DEEPER ROOT CAUSE OF THE META-CRISIS: A GLOBAL INTIMACY DISORDER

Above, I have outlined the major generator functions of existential risk. But there is a deeper cause for the existential risk that lurks underneath the rivalrous conflict governed by win/lose metrics and the fragile systems they engender.

And we cannot take the Death Star down without discerning and addressing this. We have already alluded to this root cause above, but at this point we need to make it more explicit so that, from this context, the adequate root response will become clear.

Modernity threw out the revelation, but was unable to establish a new basis for value.

This ostensibly surprising statement can be understood in a few simple steps:

1. All of the catastrophic and existential risk challenges we face are global: from climate change to artificial intelligence, pandemics, systems collapse, and exponential arms races.
2. Every global challenge self-evidently requires a global solution.
3. Global solutions can only be implemented with global co-ordination.
4. Global co-ordination is impossible without global coherence.
5. Global coherence is only possible if there is a global resonance between the parts.
6. Global resonance is only possible if we have global intimacy.

ONLY A SHARED STORY OF VALUE CAN GENERATE GLOBAL INTIMACY

Global intimacy—just like intimacy in a couple—is only possible when there is a shared story.

Not just a shared history, but a shared Story of Value.

- It is only a shared global story that can generate a new emergent quality of intimacy: global intimacy.
- A shared Story of Value must be rooted in shared ordinating values, or what we have called evolving First Values and First Principles.
- Intimacy requires a shared grammar of value as a matrix for a shared Story of Value.

The global intimacy disorder is the root cause for existential risk. The global intimacy disorder underlies the core generator functions for existential risk.

The global intimacy disorder is rooted in the failure to experience ourselves in a field of shared intrinsic value. This failure derives from the deconstruction of value.

Indeed, it is wholly accurate to say that **the root cause of the two generator functions of existential risk is the failed story of intrinsic value, or what we might also call the breakdown of Eros.**

1. The first generator function is **the success story**. Our modern success story is rivalrous conflict governed by win/lose metrics, which violates all the terms of the Intimacy Equation: there is no shared identity and no mutuality of recognition, feeling, value or purpose, and instead of *relative* otherness, there is *alienated* otherness. Such a story generates complicated fragile systems with no allurement or intimacy between the parts, systems which optimize for efficiency (as an expression of win/lose metrics) and not for resiliency and life.

2. The second generator function is **the deconstruction of intrinsic value** itself. The deconstruction of value is the sense that human value does not participate in the intrinsic value of the Real, for the Real is dogmatically declared to have no intrinsic value. Thus, there is no shared identity between the interior of the human being and Reality. There is no common participation in a field of shared intrinsic value. Instead of being intimate with value, we are alienated from value. And only intrinsic value can arouse will: political, moral, and social will.

To sum up, without a shared grammar of value there is no global intimacy, and therefore no global coherence, and no global coordination in response to catastrophic and existential risk, which means, put simply, there will be, quite literally, no future.

HEALING THE GLOBAL INTIMACY DISORDER
REQUIRES THE EVOLUTION OF INTIMACY

But we are not hopeless. On the contrary, we are filled with great hope. Hope is a memory of the future. That memory of the future *is* the direct hit that takes down the Death Star, the culture of death. **The direct hit must be**—as it has always been in history—**the emergence of a new stage of evolution.**

Crisis is an evolutionary driver, and every crisis is, at its core, a crisis of intimacy: from the oxygen crisis of the single cells dying which generated multicellular life at the dawn of existence, to the existential risk in this very moment.[9]

The direct hit is therefore structurally self-evident: the evolution of intimacy itself.

What is intimacy, as a structure of Cosmos all the way down and all the way up the evolutionary chain? We engage this inquiry in depth in other writings, but for now we will simply adduce what we have called the "Intimacy Equation":

Intimacy = shared identity in the context of [relative] otherness x *mutuality of recognition* x *mutuality of pathos* x *mutuality of value* x *mutuality of purpose*

Intimacy is about the capacity of parts to generate a *shared identity* while retaining their otherness, or distinct identity. This requires multiple mutualities, including recognition, pathos (or feeling), value, and purpose. The parts must recognize and feel each other, even as they share value and purpose. But all of this must lead to intimate union—and not pathological

---

9 We demonstrate this principle in some depth in the multi-volume series, *The Universe: A Love Story* (forthcoming) (https://worldphilosophyandreligion.org/early-ontologies), *The Intimate Universe: Global Intimacy Disorder as Cause for Global Action Paralysis* (forthcoming), and in other writings of CosmoErotic Humanism.

fusion, where the distinct identity of the parts disappears—like subatomic particles that successfully become an atom, or two people who successfully become a couple.

THE DECONSTRUCTION OF VALUE IS THE DECONSTRUCTION OF INTIMACY

We have identified the global intimacy disorder as the root cause of existential risk. But the underlying ultimate failure of intimacy is the deconstruction of value itself.

The deconstruction of value means that human value does not participate in any sense of intrinsic value of the Real. This is not about individual *values,* but about *the Field of Value* that underlies all of them. **When the human being**—moved, often sincerely or even nobly, by myriad cultural, historical, and psychological confusions—**claims to have stepped out of the Field of Value, then intimacy itself is deconstructed.**

The deconstruction of value is the deconstruction of intimacy.

In the absence of a shared Story of Value, a story that is an authentic expression of Reality's Eros, a story rooted in *pseudo-Eros* takes center stage and becomes the generator function for existential risk. Our modern pseudo-Eros story is *rivalrous conflict governed by win/lose metrics.* Such a story catalyzes in its wake the second generator function of existential risk: *complicated fragile systems with no allurement or intimacy between the parts.* It is in that sense that we have argued that the first generator function for existential risk is the success story.

- The failure of intimacy is precisely the impotent experience that there is no shared identity between the interior of the human being and Reality. **There is no shared identity in the sense of any kind of common participation in a field of shared intrinsic value.**
- **But only a shared Story of Value can arouse the global will**

required to engage catastrophic and existential risk. For it is only global political, moral, and social will—and we can even say *erotic* will—that can generate the most Good, True and Beautiful world that we have always known is possible.

THE EVOLUTION OF LOVE IS THE TELLING OF A NEW STORY

Coupled with the Intimacy Equation is the scientifically grounded realization, in both the exterior and interior sciences, that Reality is a progressive deepening of intimacies, or, said slightly differently:

Reality is Evolution. Evolution is the evolution of intimacy.

- The evolution of intimacy requires—both personally and collectively—a deeper, more accurate discernment of the nature of our universe, ourselves, and our beloveds.
- This new discernment generates a new global Story of Value.
- The new global Story of Value generates an emergent, heretofore unseen global intimacy and heals the global intimacy disorder.

The new Story of Value is the direct hit that takes down the Death Star and replaces it with the hope that invokes the memory of our best future.

Global intimacy facilitates global coherence, which facilitates global coordination, which activates the possibility of our creative and effectively coordinated global responses to the global meta-crisis in its entirety and its specific expressions.

To solve Bertrand Russell's challenge—the apparent argument for the subjectivity of ethical values—**we have to reground value theory in eternal yet evolving First Principles and First Values, and articulate a new Story of Value.**

This is what we call CosmoErotic Humanism.

CosmoErotic Humanism—together with other emergent strands—**needs to become the ground of a world religion as a context for our diversity**. We need religion, even as we need science, to articulate a shared global grammar of value.

As we said at the beginning, our choice is simple: love or die.

- To love means to participate in the evolution of love, which is the evolution of the human Story of Value.
- To love means to evolve and activate a new cultural enlightenment—rooted in a new narrative of identity, a new narrative of value, a new narrative of intimate communion, a new narrative of desire, a new narrative of power—all of which will birth new narratives of economics and politics.
- The evolution of love is the telling of a new Story.

The new Story that must be told is a love story, for in fact that is the deepest truth of Reality, rooted in the best exterior and interior sciences, that we have at this moment in time:

- Reality is not merely a fact. Reality is a story.
- Reality is not an ordinary story. Reality is a love story.
- Reality is not an ordinary love story. Reality is an Outrageous Love Story.

Story doesn't mean it's *made-up*.

It means doing the hard work of integrating the validated insights of the traditional world, the modern world, and the postmodern world.

This is the intention at the heart of telling the new Story of CosmoErotic Humanism.

ABOUT THIS VOLUME

The book begins with a conversation around public culture. How do we create an evolutionary public space that reflects our desire for a better world? How do we create coherence in a sea of social chaos? How can we move from digital abuse to digital intimacy and transform the internet into an expression of the genuine nervous system of our humanity?

This book invites us to explore elements of the necessary digital foundations for an emergent culture of Eros. This book lays down a vision for a world in which we are all evolutionary partners, awakening to the joy and responsibility of this moment in history.

Public culture is the place where we play out either the depths our private refinement or swamp of our shame. Healing the depth of our personal and cultural shame is therefore indispensable for creating a sacred public culture. As such, we explore through multiple doors the roots of our wounding and shame.

One key is to look at the way we coil, clench, and contract, guarding our hearts due to painful prior experiences. It is necessary to work with the wounds of the past, but this by itself is insufficient. This is but the first step. Through transforming and healing our shame and wounding, we liberate the driving power of activism.

Once we dis-identify with our wounding, once we stop hijacking our wounds to be the pseudo-Eros of our lives—we can then make the great leap of will into *unguarding our hearts*. It is only when we unguard our hearts that we're able to access the full power of love. We allow ourselves to be vulnerable and raw, we allow our hearts to be ripped open, we become radically tender and fierce, and we are aroused to activism. This is the path of transforming our personal and collective crisis.

Our crisis becomes a birth.

Our wounding becomes the ground of our emergence. Our wounding becomes part of the symphony of Cosmos. This new quality of symphony then generates new intimacies, which in turn open us up to new possibility It is precisely this ground of yearning intimacy—fearless in its desire and naked in its longing—that defines the quality of Outrageous Love. We don't need to be perfect, but we need to allow ourselves to make mistakes in the right direction. We are all a holy and a broken *Hallelujah*. Our wounding is the weave of our wonder.

To fully access our potential, we need to liberate shame—for shame is the root of all evil. Shame is the devastating experience that we can't be fixed.

Shame's distorted energy plays out as envy, projection, and demonization, with extremely destructive consequences both in the private and public space.

Instead of allowing shame to shrink and cripple us, we need to liberate shame by first listening to it and confessing it. But then—listening more deeply to its strangely seductive beckoning—shame is whispering: *You are a King! You are a Queen!* Shame only makes sense if we understand that on some level, we are only shamed *because* we are kings and queens. It is only from this place that we can say, "Shame on you, such behavior does not befit your royalty, your depth, your goodness, your truth."

From this place of royal dignity, I have the ground and capacity to be vulnerable—to unguard my heart to myself and others. I stop my knee-jerk perception of myself and others as victims or perpetrators. I recover my capacity to see people as good and even gorgeous expressions of Reality's ever uniquely radiant flowerings. At the same time, I hold myself and others accountable. I call myself and others to face and transform the shadow and rise to our true, unique greatness. This process of transformation into Unique Self is love in action itself.

Living your Unique Self is an affront to shame. Only when we live our Unique Self can we be in devotion to someone else's Unique Self. Only from the place of my Unique Self can I be delighted by the uniqueness of someone else.

When we are really in our Unique Self, we have all the room in the world to be generous, loving, and excited by the unique gifts of others. We are allured to *join genius* and to create more and ever greater Unique Self Symphonies. There is no greater joy than to know that I am the right person in the right place at the right time. Joy and happiness cannot be pursued. Rather, joy is the byproduct of the passionate pursuit of living my Unique Self and giving my unique gift.

We are called to raise our voices for a better tomorrow. We raise our voices for tenderness and for kindness. We unguard our hearts and become evolutionary activists. We begin by creating small islands of coherence, which then ripple out into culture. Being together as Outrageous Lovers, as evolutionary mystics, as Unique Selves in Unique Self Symphonies, is the seedbed of a new culture of love.

Love is not hard to find—love is impossible to avoid. Love animates and suffuses Reality in every second, as we live in The Universe: A Love Story.

Volume 5

These oral essays are edited talks delivered by Marc Gafni and Barbara Marx Hubbard between August and October 2017.

ABOUT THIS VOLUME

CHAPTER ONE

TO EVOLVE PUBLIC CULTURE
WE MUST EVOLVE OUR SHAME

Episode 41 — August 5, 2017

WE ARE LEARNING TO BE GOOD GODS

We are dealing with a very deep issue of public culture: secrecy versus privacy.

If you keep something secret, you are holding it within as though there is something wrong. There is a feeling of shame; there is a feeling you can be criticized.

Whereas if you hold it in private—whether it is something inside yourself that you feel you have done wrong, or you hold it in private between two or more people where you all feel it can be misinterpreted—it makes a huge difference as to how it goes.

I invite everyone in resonance to take a moment to examine that within ourselves and ask: *Do we have anywhere inside a secret that brings us shame, brings us fear, brings us humiliation?* Just allow yourself to consider anything of that nature that might be within, and then take that pain, sorrow, shame, secret and bring it into the privacy of your heart

where you are safe, where you are understood, where your ego is not in charge. You may feel regretful, but you don't feel ashamed, humiliated, destroyed. The learning for us as we are becoming universal humans, *Homo universalis*, quite literally with the powers of gods, of our ancient gods, our ancient mythological gods, is to realize we have these powers now. **The time has come to completely clean up the inner act.**

Let's everyone take whatever there might be of a painful experience that you have kept secret and bring it into a private place in your heart where your egoic nature is not criticizing you for it. At the same time, you are able to share it either just within yourself or with another and feel the release of that.

Let's project that onto public culture, because some of the things that people have done that they are keeping secret are very destructive. Imagine them bringing it out into private space internally and with others and see if the fear and rejection and destructive behavior is somewhat mitigated at least. **As we're becoming *Homo universalis* with the powers we used to call the powers of gods, we really are learning to be good gods.** Just like Jesus said, *Don't you know that you are gods? You will do the work that I do, and greater works than these will you do in the fullness of time.* So be it.

WE ARE AT A MOMENT OF PHASE SHIFT IN HUMANITY

Amen, amen, amen. Welcome, everyone. We are in the very beginning, my friends, of Evolutionary Church. We are just getting started. We are here together to awaken the new species. We are here to become the new human.

We share this every week, and we share it every place we can in the world with everyone, but the seedbed, the source, is us together. **The seedbed is being together here in Evolutionary Church and saying and speaking: *We are evolution*!** We are evolution. I am evolution. I don't exist without you.

I don't exist without Evolutionary Church. I am because you are. All of us exist in the context of each other. Particularly here in Evolutionary Church, we are coming together. We are coming together as they came together in Bethlehem at this pivotal moment in history, which is demanding a new vision, which is not just a technical series of small minor fluctuations.

> *We are at a moment which is a phase shift in humanity: either we are going to arise and evolve, or we will regress and deconstruct causing untold suffering.*

At this pivoting point, the Evolutionary Church comes together, and we love each other outrageously, not with ordinary love—but with Outrageous Love. We cry out every week with delight, with rapture, but also with grounded dignity, with deep insight, with wild and profound grounded love for each other, and we say:

> *We live in a world of outrageous pain, and the only response to outrageous pain is Outrageous Love, is Evolutionary Love.*

Evolutionary Love means that at the core of everything is Eros, is love. Love is the movement towards contact. It is an experience. Eros and love are the same word.

Eros is the experience of being radically alive, moving towards ever greater contact and creativity.

That is what I call Outrageous Love, or Evolutionary Love. This is part of our language—our field of new language here in church. In order to change the source code, to shift and awaken a new species, to become together the new human and incarnate the new human, we need the *Logos*. As the *Good*

*Book—The Book of John—*says, we need *the Word.* We need the new word, and the new word is the new field of language.

Abracadabra! Abracadabra is, in Aramaic: *a'brah ke'a'dab'ra:* "I speak, and I create."

By speaking a new language, by laying down a new field of language, by laying down a new set of distinctions, and here in Evolutionary Church, incarnating those distinctions together, oh my God, we make magic! We wave the wand like they did in the beginning of the Renaissance, and we create the new human. We become the new human. We incarnate the new human.

We become the new *Christos* or the new Buddha or the new global evolutionary citizen when we align with that evolutionary impulse of Eros living in us, as us, and through us. What a delight to be here. Welcome, welcome everyone.

It is a core structure that I have been talking about in various ways for a few decades. It is core to what we think and breathe here in Evolutionary Church, and what *do* we think and breathe?

We know that every time we are acting out—every breakdown in ethics is a failure of Eros, it is a failure of love.

When I know that: I am chosen, I am intended, I am desired, I am recognized, I am adored, and I am needed

These are the six core human needs—not just by one other individual, but by All-That-Is. When I know that, then my ethics play out. Then I move to change the world. Then I'm excited.

OUR NEW CREDO: WE ARE EVOLUTION

We come together like we do every week in prayer. We are going to go in and feel into our friend, Leonard Cohen, who speaks about *bringing the broken vessels.* What are the broken vessels? In the original Hebrew lineage—where Leonard Cohen's song, *Hallelujah,* comes from—in the original great lineage of Kabbalah, we speak about the divine light that penetrates Reality and organizes itself in ten vessels, and those vessels have too much light. The light is too intense. The vessels can't contain the light, so the vessels shatter. And those shattered vessels, we all know from our own lives, those shattered vessels are the broken *Hallelujahs,* and what Cohen sings so beautifully is that the shattered vessels are not an accident of Cosmos.

The shattered vessels of our lives are the holy and the broken Hallelujah.

Every breath we draw is *Hallelujah.* We offer it all up at the altar, the altar of God, who is not merely the Infinity of Power, not the Santa Claus god, but the God who is the Infinity of Intimacy, who knows our name, into whose arms we fall, and remember in Evolutionary Church, my beloved brothers and sisters, we are evolving the source code, and we say, the god you don't believe in doesn't exist. **We are evolving the Divine. The Divine in us evolves God, evolves the word.** God is the Infinity of Intimacy into whose arms we fall as She holds us in all of our holy and broken *Hallelujahs.* And every holy and broken *Hallelujah,* every secret of a broken *Hallelujah,* every secret can be shared in a way that is appropriate with people that are appropriate, and I can be loved through. We have to first release shame.

Let's hold on to guilt. We like guilt. Guilt means accountability. We are all accountable, and to be accountable, it just means, we made a mistake. We own it. We correct it the best we can. We make amends the best we can, and we move on reclaiming our innocence again:

- Everything can be fixed.
- Everything can be resolved.
- Everything can be recreated.
- Everything can be transformed.

We bring with delight, with pain, with rapture, with resonance, with ecstasy, we bring before the Mother, before the Divine, before the Infinity of Intimacy, we bring the holy and the broken *Hallelujah*.

We're at Evolutionary Church, offering up our prayers as we do every week: the holy and the broken *Hallelujah. Amen.* Yes!

We offer prayer, to evolve prayer and to create prayer. We have lost prayer, so, we offer up and we say, *God, help me! Help me with making a living! Help me be the person that I want to be! Help me show up, help me wake up, help me grow up! Help my uncle Morris, who has cancer and who needs an operation.* We go, and we say: *Prayer affirms the dignity of personal need.* Then we pray for everything, and we ask for everything because we are the Infinity of Intimacy and the Infinity of Intimacy, God, in the second person holds us and knows us.

I invite everyone to speak your prayers, all the gates are opening, and we turn to God; not the god we don't believe in, but the God who is the Infinity of Intimacy who knows our name, and we offer up prayer. Oh my God!

Friends, we are here in Evolutionary Church—we are here evolving the source code together. We are evolution. As we come together and we awaken ourselves, and as we reclaim prayer, we reclaim a relationship to God who knows our name, who is the Infinity of Intimacy, and who lives in us, as us, and through us at the same time.

We are Rumi falling into the arms of the Beloved and yet awakening as God/Goddess in the very same moment. We hold that not as contradiction, but as holy paradox.

We are evolution! Anyone who thinks that we are evolution, as we are now in the beginning of church, let's just write: *I am evolution.* Once you feel *I am evolution,* then let's write: *We are evolution together,* because we, in Evolutionary Church, are taking responsibility for evolving the source code. I am evolution! We cry it out. *We are evolution.* I am! Don't just sit back, my friends. This is not a spectator event. As we write it, it becomes

6

true. *I am evolution. We are evolution.* We are awakening the new species right here.

To bring this down into reality, we are awakening the new species. We are Bethlehem. We are not waiting for someone else to do it. Everyone is invited. Evolutionary Church belongs to all of us. *I am evolution*, the new credo of Evolutionary Church. We are going to become the new human. We are going to awaken the new humanity. I am evolution. We are evolution.

In this unique WeSpace, oh my God, we are all evolving. I am evolution. You get the difference, my friends?

If we are in a biology department at a college—whether it is MIT or whether it is a prep school like Exeter, or whether it is PS141 in the Bronx—we teach evolution as a theory. It is a theory of how mutation works and it is a technical process and it is something that is out there. That misunderstands evolution, my friends! *We are evolution!*

We are evolution means that:

- Reality is not a fact; it is a story.
- It is not an ordinary story; it is a love story.
- It is not an ordinary love story; it is an Evolutionary Love story.
- It is an Outrageous Love Story.

And who is evolution?

Each one of us is evolution. We *are* the new species. We are not waiting to invoke the new species in someone else; we are not preaching to anyone. We are *being* it. We *are* evolution. We *incarnate* the impulse. Let's stop the fight with ego, everyone. Let's do something even more dramatic and beautiful and bold and simple.

> *Let's stop the historical fight with ego. We have to do one thing: align with the evolutionary impulse!*

We align with the evolutionary impulse. We see with God's eyes. **That's what it means to be a lover. It is to see with God's eyes.** We are evolution. We are laying down the tracks of the new human and the new humanity.

WHEN YOU FEEL THE PAIN THE WHOLE WAY, IT DISSIPATES

One of the issues we need to address—and one of the things we work with together here in Evolutionary Church—is that it needs to be grounded. It's not just declaring; it's grounded. We are rising up, but we are like Jacob's ladder: a ladder rooted in the ground and rising up into the heavens. To root us in the ground, every week we have a *dharma*—a message, a teaching of evolving public culture.

How do we create a public space, which is evolution? How do we create an evolutionary public space, an evolutionary space where we learn how to love each other? We learn what to share and what not to share. What is holy privacy? What needs to be transparent? In our message, we want to talk about secrets:

- What is the difference between secrets sacred and secrets sordid?
- What is the difference between sacred privacy and holy transparency?
- What should we share?
- What should we hold close?
- Is it important to hold things close?
- Should all secrets be shared?

8

This is part of how we hold each other and how we hold our public culture. We are evolving public culture together.

We are creating a space in which we move from digital abuse to digital intimacy because the internet is the nervous system of our planet. How do we take that nervous system of our planet and evolve it, wake it up, and infuse it with Evolutionary Love?

We are the opposite of the Tower of Babel. *Amen.*

We are talking about secrecy and privacy, that comes from the work of A.H. Almaas in his book, *Essence.*[1] It has to do with what you do when you are feeling a pain that is so distressing to you that either you hide it in secrecy or—if you're lucky—you might share it in private, but it doesn't get rid of it. We all have these moments of distress, of pain, of regret, and sometimes it lodges itself in our hearts and can cause tremendous problems of every kind, physical, mental, and spiritual. I want to read you something about the Almaas presentation from my (Barbara's) book *Emergence,*[2] and then try it out.

> Almaas suggests that whenever we feel anything that is deficient, hurts, or painful, we directly experience the deficiencies of ego and recognize that what the ego is attempting to do is already present in essence. The process here is to feel deeply ego's lack or hole.

It is about something that is really distressing to you. Let's say that for me it was fear of failure. I had all of these tremendous things to do; I'm a compulsive workaholic, and I couldn't feel like I was succeeding no matter what I did. This is fear of failure.

> The process here is to feel this lack as a whole and not defend against this feeling or lack, nor come up with any strategies for solving the problem from the egoic point of view.

---

1 A.H. Almaas, *Essence with The Elixir of Enlightenment: The Diamond Approach to Inner Realization.*

2 Barbara Marx Hubbard, *Emergence: The Shift from Ego to Essence.*

From the egoic point of view, it would be to work harder, work better, work with somebody else. For me it was an endless cycle. Here are the steps we take:

First, the Beloved.

The Beloved is whatever you call your true Essential Self, your God Self, your Source.

> The Beloved invites the local selves to come forward and describe as deeply as possible any pain or deficiency being experienced.

This is really dealing with the inner secrecy where we hold things in pain and bring it out in private to get the full story of it:

> The needs, the wants, the pain. Don't defend against the experience. Don't try to fix it or solve it from the egoic point of view, but rather completely allow the pain to be present, to identify within yourself something that distresses you about yourself and about your place in the world.

And let's feel it the whole way in private. We don't need to share this with everybody.

> Feel its location in the body, its density, its vibration. Second, we stay with that pain and follow it all the way through the root, to the source where we first felt such pain.

Whatever that pain is. In my case I'm thinking of failure as the one that has plagued me. I go back to where I first felt it, and I think it was with my father. He said to me, *Barbara, you are a crazy fool, and you are 100% right.* That was the big signal I got from my father, but it hurt because I wanted to please him. So, stay with that pain, whatever it is, be it the fear of failure, the fear of inadequacy, the fear of mistakes. **Stay with the fear of whatever it is and say,** *let's go the whole way in***, in private, but not in secret**. That is how we bring it out, and according to Almaas:

> When we follow the deficiency as deeply as possible, it leads us to that part of Essence or the Beloved or the Source that the local

10

self has been seeking by trying to have some strategy in the outer world.

If it is feeling a fear of failure and you're trying to get over that by succeeding in the outer world, that's an endless process, so you feel the failure. Go all the way in until you feel the deficiency deeply.

And then you let our local selves discover that the fulfillment they have been seeking is already present in the Beloved.

You are the Beloved Source, and when your fear of failure, your fear of whatever it is, is allowed to go totally into that, the fear dissipates. He describes it:

When you allow yourself quietly to experience the hurtful wound and memories connected with it, whatever the experience is.

You have to really feel it all the way, the hurtful feelings. Wow, there is so much pain!

The golden elixir will flow out of it, healing and filling the emptiness with the beautiful, sweet fullness that will melt the heart.

In my case, if I go into the fear of failure, and I think of this well-motivated girl wanting to please her father and wanting to find out the meaning of our power and all of that—she is adorable! You get to feel her that way.

The golden elixir will flow out of it, healing and filling the emptiness with the beautiful, sweet fullness that will melt the heart, erase the mind and bring about the contentment that the individual has been thirsting for.

It comes from your own Beloved, internal being-self, God Self. When you bring it all the way in, you have to feel it all the way—not try to protect yourself from it—because it is by feeling it the whole way that the God Self, whatever we wish to call it, our sourcing-self, is able to heal it. Not even only that. It gives you the contentment that the ego has been seeking. Let's say the contentment in fear of failure is: *I am succeeding in something, whatever it might be.* Well, from the point of view of my God Self, as this created being that is doing her best—the God Self is totally appreciative already.

We have been saying in the church: *Confess your greatness.* It is also: *confess God's love of you in your expression and your efforts.* God's complete sanctioning of that effort within you is where the source of your comfort comes from.

> Ego's search for satisfaction is over, says Almaas, because your not-defending and not-strategizing leads you to that part of the Pearl—which is capital P—which he called "Essence," that which it has been seeking through strategizing.

Let's take this in terms of dealing with secrecy and privacy and all the slander and all the destruction of one another that is going on by way of criticism in our current society—and take it all in—instead of reacting against this one or that one for their outrageous behavior. Go into that source of the Beloved where they are striving so much to win, to prevail, to do well and just on behalf of them, as well as of yourself, the people who are trying to prevail in this world, take it all into the essence. Feel the almost tenderness of God for the striving of humanity, to prevail and to be the best and to win and to have power. Wow.

Let's take it all in, in the privacy of our heart, in the safety of our Source, in the security of our Evolutionary Church. **Our Evolutionary Church is a seedbed for the new human, that it is a learning ground for the evolutionary *Homo universalis* to become self-aware.** Every feeling that hurts, that is painful, that is upsetting, or that is beautiful, glorious, and wonderful is welcome here. Let's nurture it in the field of the emerging human, and let's imagine ourselves becoming that. Do it day by day— whatever your feelings are—take them within to Source. Let that Source of Essential Self express itself with all the dignity and beauty that is in it, to give its gift, to be loved and to love. That is the source of it all.

We are going to learn how to do this together. Although I haven't yet dealt with the public-culture aspect of the difference between secrecy and privacy, I wanted to address it on a deep psychological level. Let's take all the pain into Source. Let it be healed at the source of God within, of Source within, of love within, of the Beloved within, of the Essential Self within. Let's come out with the capacity to love, to forgive, and to co-create at the scale that is needed for *Homo universalis.*

BY CONFESSING MY SHAME, IT IS RELEASED

We need to find a way to liberate shame. **Shame is the root of all evil.**

Let's understand that. Almaas, in his lovely book *Essence,* expresses one dimension of this—the psychological dimension. Let's go from the beginning. Let's walk, and we have to walk three more steps here in order to get home. Almaas takes us the first gorgeous step. Then we will go the next two, three steps.

What is the first step? The first step is shame.

- Shame comes from secrets that need to be shared that aren't shared.
- Shame comes from the gap between the experience of who I would like to be, from the gap between the experience of who I project into the world, and who in my heart of hearts, I believe that I really am.

Why do I believe that I'm really not the person that I say I am or that I project into the public? Many of us have hidden secrets, hidden stories, which we are afraid that if we shared, we wouldn't be loved. *If they really knew who I was, if they really knew what I did, if they really knew my violation, they wouldn't love me.* So, Almaas and Barbara speak to this beautiful idea, which Brené Brown also speaks about beautifully, that the secrets need to be shared.

Barbara, in her book *Emergence*, takes it the next step and says:

> *I need to really understand that all my acting out comes from striving, from a desire to show up, from a desire to be recognized, from a desire to be noticed. I realize that all of my striving is rooted in this core, deep, and profound desire to be loved, to be seen. Then I feel that I am loved, and I know that I am seen, and I know that I am recognized, and in that knowing, I can release my shame. In that knowing, I can share my secret, be loved through my secret, and be honored through my secret.*

It doesn't mean I am not accountable, but *I am* accountable. **I am accountable because that is my dignity.** My dignity is to make amends in any way and transform any hurt that I might have done, and at the same time, I am always held by the Divine, radically loved, radically honored, radically recognized.

Even my sin was part of the Divine intention. Even my fall was part of the intention of the Divine who created beings who would be exiled from Eden because the job of the human being is to embrace their holy and broken *Hallelujah,* and God knew and Reality knew that we would fall from Eden.

The fall from Eden wasn't a mistake. It was the intention of the Cosmos itself.

Shame is the primary wound in which we forget our glory. We forget our innocence. We forget our goodness.

Shame is the experience that we can't be fixed. **Shame is the experience that we came from the factory broken, and that broken part is not being manufactured anymore.**

The first step beyond shame is to find that part of shame that comes from the secrets that haven't been shared. This is not going to take us home yet. This is step one, what Barbara said was so beautiful, so important: it is the critical first step.

14

But before we go to the next step, let's do the first step together. I want to invite everyone to do something kind of really daring, okay? Really, really daring: the sharing of shame.

Let's confess our shame. Share a secret, or if it is inappropriate, we will just say, *I am sharing my shame* and *I am confessing my shame* or *I am confessing my vulnerability.*

I want to invite everyone to a confession of vulnerability, and the vulnerability might be a secret I want to share, or I might not want to share the actual secret, I might just want to say, *I confess my shame,* and we love everyone. Are we willing to say, *I confess my shame*? When we try and confess our shame, it is liberated. **By confessing my shame, it is released**.

We are going to go a next huge step in healing shame, but before that, are we willing to say, *I confess my shame?* I don't have to share the details. I can, but can I confess my secret? *I confess my secret.* Let's confess our shame with the holy delight of having it received here.

Now, friends, let's take it the next step, let's go the next step. What is the secret of shame? Shame is whispering a secret in our ear, and, friends, we have to be careful of shaming shame because *Reality is a trickster.* Deep within shame there is a door. Let's now take it beyond Almaas. Almaas goes the first step, and I love his book, *Essence,* and it is beautiful, but we have to go way beyond there because **this first step of confessing my shame won't yet take us home.** It is a first step. It is a beautiful first step, but now I have to take me home.

I am going to confess my shame. The secret of my shame is whispering to me. Let me try and tell you a little bit of a secret. I am going to whisper now, okay, so no one else hears.

Okay, here is the whisper: imagine that you are a gas station attendant. Now, being a gas station attendant is a beautiful job. It is reliable, it is steady, it provides a service. You can interact with people. It is a proud and beautiful job.

But imagine that before you were a gas station attendant, you were the king. You were the king of the world. That was your job. You were born into royalty. You were the king, and all of a sudden you found yourself a gas station attendant. Well, then you would be ashamed. Why? Because a gas station attendant is not your Unique Self. It is not your greatness. It is not your gift; it is not your contribution! **Shame only makes sense if I've forgotten that I am a king.**

You see, shame also can't be shamed. We have to be careful of shaming shame. See, underneath what Almaas said and underneath the beauty that Barbara brought us there is this essential next step. When Barbara and I talked about it, we said—*Barbara's going to go the first step, and I'm going to go the second step.* We are in deep whole mate partnership here. Barbara went the first step gorgeously. We confess our shame, but now we have confessed our shame, we realize that our shame is whispering something in our ear.

SHAME IS WHISPERING: *YOU ARE A KING!*

Our shame is whispering in our ear, *you are a king!* You are only ashamed to be a gas station attendant if you remember that you are a king.

I'm only ashamed if I am great. If I am a worm, there is nothing to be ashamed of. But if my gifts could change the world and the world needs my gifts desperately, which is in fact the truth of being a Unique Self, then my shame whispers in my ear, *I love you. You are awesome.*

My shame whispers to me of my greatness. Now, my friends, feel your shame, feel my shame. And my shame says to me:

> Marc, you are innocent, you are gorgeous. You are fully accountable, you are great, and you have a great contribution to make. You were born to awaken the new species and to incarnate the new human and to call for the new humanity together with

Kristina and together with Terry and together with Barbara and together with all of us whole mates.

So, friends, listen to shame whispering, and now let's confess our greatness.

We confess the gift that is ours to give, and we move from shame to greatness. I confess my greatness. **I confess my greatness because shame reminds me of my greatness.** Shame alerts me that I have separated from Source—though actually, I'm part of Source all the time. Shame reminds me that Divinity lives in me, as me, and through me. So, I confess my greatness. I confess the greatness of my integrity. When you confess your greatness, add something on about your unique gift. What is the greatness of your unique gift?

EVERY TRUTH HAS ITS TEMPLE: DISTINGUISHING SECRET SORDID AND SECRET SACRED

And from that place, my friends, let's bring this back. Yes, yes, and yes to secrecy, and transparency. It is so deep, the secret thing.

What happens when we tell someone a secret? What do they immediately do? They go to share it with someone else. When someone says, *I'm going to keep your secret*, what they mean is, I'm not going to tell anyone except for the two people I tell.

Why is it so hard for people to keep a secret?

Some secrets should be kept. Privacy is legitimate: to be an initiate in a great tradition, for example. Secrets are not only secrets sordid, like the terrible secret of abuse. The terrible secret of behavior that needs to be brought to the light of day, so it can be stopped, so we can prevent that anyone is not being honored in their full human dignity.

Those are secrets sordid, but there are also secrets sacred.

There are secrets that are so holy, they can't be shared, obviously.

Why then, when we share with someone a secret of ours, do they go to tell it to someone else immediately, at least to one or two people? Do you remember having shared a secret that you shouldn't have?

The reason we share a secret, and let's invite ourselves to move beyond that, the reason we share a secret that shouldn't be shared is because we love the hit of attention energy we get when we share the secret. We crave that attention. When we share a secret with someone and they give us all their attention as we share the secret, we feel affirmed in the attention we are receiving.

That is why in every mystical tradition, the ability to hold a secret, a sacred secret, a holy privacy—not a wrong secret, not a secret sordid, but a secret sacred—is essential.

You can only be an initiate, a member of a great tradition, of a holy society when you can hold a secret because it means that you have enough of an inner center that you know your greatness, that you have confessed your greatness and that you can find your greatness within yourself so you don't need to get it by sharing the secret.

That's a big deal!

So now I want to welcome privacy in our space. I want to welcome privacy, my friends. **I want to welcome the dignity of privacy.** I want to say even more than that. Yes, there are secrets that need to be confessed, but there are also those things we confess only before God.

There is even a certain dimension that we confess only to our closest friends, and that is our greatness. There is a true dimension of the true greatness we have that is so dazzling the world can't even handle it. There is always that which we only share with those in our most intimate circle, and that is beautiful. That is beautiful, that is gorgeous. You know why? **When we just share the fact without the whole context, we are actually lying**. Now, the next thought is really deep. See if you can follow this with me. It is really deep: in modernity and postmodernity, we say everything should be transparent. But that is not true.

Not everything should be transparent. *Don't throw pearls before swine!* **Every truth has its temple.** You get that? Every truth has its temple. You have to know what temple your truth is for. When someone shares with you a secret sacred, you hold that with such dignity. You hold that with such honor, you hold that with such delight.

Every truth has its temple. We have to beware of this culture that says make everything transparent.

Privacy has an enormous dignity. So, let's know what to share. Let's release and liberate shame of all secrets that are secrets that I feel. *If I don't share that and realize that people love me even though I'm sharing that—I won't be able to love myself.* Then share it and find the right place to share it and the right person to share it with because every truth has its temple.

Let's confess our greatness, so that we can hold other people's holy secrets, so that we don't need to be inappropriately transparent, so that we realize that inappropriate transparency is a lie, because in inappropriate transparency, I can only share the facts, not the context.

If postmodernity taught us anything, it is that context matters. Does everyone get it? It is so deep. **Postmodernity tells us two things: be transparent about everything, and context matters. But those two things contradict each other!** If context matters—and when you share, you can only share the fact—then by just sharing the fact you are lying because without the full context, you are not really sharing the depth of the secret. Wow! Does everyone get this evolution of the *dharma*? We just changed the source code here! We love Almaas. Almaas was a great start, and Barbara took us the first critical step that we need. We go that first gorgeous step, and then we go from there:

- The first step is that we have to share the secrets that are sordid. We have to share the secrets that are blocking us from our ability to feel loved by our close beloveds. Let's share those secrets in the right way. Every truth has its temple.
- And number two—let's hold the dignity of privacy, the dignity of the Holy of Holies in the Temple, which you weren't allowed to enter at any time and in any place.

There is a reason we don't go around naked. **The reason we don't go around naked is not because we are ashamed of our nakedness, but because our full nakedness, our full emotional nakedness and our full physical nakedness requires a context.** Every truth has its temple.

Owning and evolving public culture and making this real distinction between privacy, which is sacred, and inappropriate secrecy, between *secrets sacred* and *secrets sordid*, evolves the source code and liberates shame for real. Do you have a secret that you hold only to yourself and one close friend? Beautiful. Nothing to be ashamed of. You get it? That's a holy privacy if it is a secret sacred.

So, yes, yes! We are here together, my friends, to liberate shame. We are here together to know that we are the new species. We are evolution. Let's finish and listen to Libby Roderick as she sings and we write one last time: *I am evolution.*

As Libby Roderick sings, we sing to each other.

"How Could Anyone?" Libby Roderick [See Appendix].

CHAPTER TWO

WE ARE AROUSED TO ACTIVISM WITH AN UNGUARDED HEART

Episode 42 — August 12, 2017

OUR LOVE TURNS ON THE NOOSPHERE

Welcome everyone to the Evolutionary Church of Co-creation. Let's assemble in the midst of the sea of social chaos. Let's place our coherent expression of love and evolutionary potential into the field of social chaos of our planetary society. Let's just place it in the noosphere, the thinking layer of Earth, the planetary nervous system. I invite you to go within and access the deepest impulse of creative love inside of you, wherever and however you feel it. I am feeling it myself. Feel that which most deeply attracts you to give and to express.

Feel the love going up into the noosphere, into the thinking layer of Earth, into the planetary nervous system, and recognize that that system is sensitive to the impulse of love.

It's like the nervous system of a newborn baby is sensitive to the impulse of love. When that baby is crying, the key is to be held in the arms of its mother, and quickly it opens its eyes and smiles. The miracle of the newborn baby

could be seen in our resonance as the miracle of the newborn planetary organism.

How many evolutionary impulses of love, creativity, oneness, and wholeness does our nervous system need to turn on?

I declare that we will be part of that turning on of our nervous system.

We will be the holy hosts of the planetary awakening. We are a church for the co-creation of humanity. There is no other church yet like this.

Every one of us is an impulse of evolution, attracted to the planetary awakening in love through the Unique Self Symphony of each of our voices.

There is a very powerful thought that I will refer to later, which is, there is new scientific research that informs us that DNA affects Reality. It's not only your inner impulse, your purpose, and your offering of your love; it's your very DNA code.

When you're in a certain state of being, your DNA code affects other DNA codes all on its own. I have felt that to be true in joining genius. Place your attention on your DNA, the frequency of the design of your unique organism, and infuse that DNA with love of the expression of the organism that it has created, and then it connects with the DNA of everybody in this church. Let us experience our DNA connecting.

KNOWING THAT WE ARE THE NEW RENAISSANCE CREATES AROUSAL

What a delight. I am filled with delight. Can everyone feel delight? We are here in the new Bethlehem. This is the new Bethlehem here, and it is filled with meaning:

22

We can arise as the new human.

We can arise as the new humanity.

It's our turn.

All of Reality waits, *literally.*

I want to put my absolute promise and knowing on this. Reality literally waits for us here and says: *give me a new church, a new synagogue, a new mosque, a new vision of Spirit which tells the new story, which awakens the new species.*

We are the new Renaissance. It is us! It's our turn! **Knowing that we are the new Renaissance is so powerful and creates such an arousal, such a delight.**

You know we talked before about this process of joining genius and the exciting arousal in it. My friends, we have exiled arousal!

All that arousal means to us nowadays, is that for a quick moment we got sexually aroused and then we are all confused because it does not come back again; and we are lost for answers—*what are we going to do, how are we gonna handle it?* Then we go to therapy, and we try to work it out, but that is the exile of arousal.

Blessings to the sexual, but that is not our topic in this talk here. What we are here to talk about is what the sexual models.

The sexual models Eros, which is true arousal. Arousal means I am so moved by this moment, and I am awakening into this moment.

I (Marc) was aroused when I saw our new icon for church filled with mystical meaning. What aroused me was not just the objective meaning of the new icon for church, it was the pouring of someone's intention and love into it, that is creating the structure of this church. That aroused me.

When I heard Barbara finding the resonant field, I said, *Oh my God, Barbara Marx Hubbard, you are such a rock star!* And I was just aroused. What a privilege. When I look at all the names of people here in Church from everywhere, when I see the countries from all over the world, it is so fantastic to see that, and I say, *I am aroused.*

We are the Outrageous Lovers. This is our moment. Feel that privilege! If I think, *Oh we are just going to do church today.* Really? No, not *just* church! It's a new moment; it's a new time! It's a privilege.

The *dharma*, the memetic structures, the source code changing structures that we are articulating here together in Evolutionary Church, are as powerful as the source code changing structures that Leonardo da Vinci with his circle articulated in Florence, Italy that began the Renaissance.

A CORE STRUCTURE OF THE UNIVERSE: AROUSAL FROM ABOVE, AROUSAL FROM BELOW

We are arising! We are arising and let us feel that power of arousal coursing through us. There is a text and this beautiful idea in Hebrew mysticism, that says that we get a gift from God which is *it'aruta d'l'eilah*—or "arousal from above." Isn't that beautiful? Arousal from above! It is a gift:

- The first ten weeks of Evolutionary Church: That is arousal from above.
- I am doing an *Arise Festival*: That is arousal from above.
- At the beginning of joining genius: That is arousal from above.
- It is when I fall in love: That is arousal from above.

It is a free gift. It is a gift from the universe. **Arousal from above is what happens when we fall in love.** You fall in love with someone and, *oh my*

God, I'm in love! My friend who I'm in love with, says to me: *Hey, honey, do you want to see a movie?* And I say: *Sure!* They say: *What movie do you want to see?* And I say to them, *Honey, as long as we are together, it doesn't matter.* That's arousal from above, and then what happens is—it happens with all of us, friends—we lose it because that's the structure of the universe.

Arousal from above is a gift from God.

The structure of the universe is: we get a gift, which is arousal from above. If we are really going to change the source code, if we are really going to transform at all, we have to claim what the Hebrew mystics call *it'aruta d'l'tata*, arousal from below.

Arousal from below is doing the work.

We claim it. We claim it, and Barbara, when I (Marc) feel into your steadiness, your depth, and when I wait for my letters every morning and I send back and write: *Hey, I am writing now, but I am going to write in the evening.* We have this depth of years of writing. Then we feel our beloved whole mate holder of space and evolutionary teacher here working hard to make Evolutionary Church and to create sacred space. I feel everyone coming together after so many weeks in Evolutionary Church:

- This is arousal from below.
- This is where we meet God.
- This is where we meet Goddess.
- This is where we evolve what it means to pray.
- This is where we say that the god you don't believe in doesn't exist, for the forty-second time.

We have been doing this for two years; we have expanded and now have 5,000 people in Evolutionary Church, but it is not enough. We need five million people so that when Evolutionary Church rises up, it says to President Trump, *Hello, that is not okay,* and it says to North Korea, *Hey guys, come to church.*

We have to become a force. We have to move from a trickle to a trickle that is increasing in speed and depth until it becomes a torrent—a torrential river flowing to an ocean of depth, which is Evolutionary Church, synagogue, mosque, temple, where *we are being the new human*. Where we love each other outrageously and unabashedly. We are not afraid to love each other. We are not afraid to live out loud in love and remember Solomon, the great Song of Songs, who wrote, *Its insides are lined with love.*

GOD WANTS US TO BRING EVERYTHING TO PRAYER

The only way we can be lovers, the only way we can be Evolutionary Lovers, the only way we can be Outrageous Lovers is if we bring it all. Nothing's left out. We come before the Divine and we say: *I am going to bring everything* because every word drawn from our lips is *Hallelujah.*

What does *Hallelujah* mean, the hymn that we sing every week? *Hallelujah* means pristine gorgeous praise, and *Hallelujah* also means my broken moments, my drunken intoxication. We realize that whenever we are on our knees, we are always on our knees to God. We know that this is true, it is not a word. We realize I am evolution awakening as me, in me, and through me. I can't wait to be aroused by our sermon today. We're going to shift the source code, and we're going to have comments, and we're going to have prayers.

I woke up this morning scared. I didn't even know why. Sometimes we wake up in the morning scared. I'm a powerful human being, and I woke up scared this morning. **I bring that being scared to church, and I put it on the altar, the holy and the broken *Hallelujah*, and from that place we are Outrageous Lovers.**

Friends, let's open our hearts. We are going to offer our prayers to God, and the god you don't believe in doesn't exist. Who is the God that we are speaking to? Let's shut our eyes for a second and access the God who affirms the dignity of personal need because prayer affirms the full dignity of personal need.

26

My (Marc's) lineage teacher, the Baal Shem Tov, whom Buber wrote about in his *Tales of Hasidism*, the Master of the Good Name, he would say: *Ask for everything!* When we pray, we ask for everything, and who will we be praying to? Not to the Santa Claus god, but to the God who is the Infinity of Intimacy. God is not just the Infinity of Power, God is the Infinity of Intimacy.

We are going to shut our eyes for a second and imagine what we call *God in the third person*, which is the infinite laws of physics, the laws of mathematics, all of the power, the supernovas of Reality, all of the calculus, all of the laws of chemistry, mitosis, meiosis, photosynthesis, hundreds of billions and billions of years, light-years, power complexity dazzling wisdom beyond imagination, beauty beyond imagination, that all the super computers and every scientist in every generation couldn't even vaguely imagine, the twinkle of an eye, all of that power and all of that genius beyond genius for which we have no words—the Infinity of Brilliance, Infinity of Power, God in the third person. **That is the third person, the God who is ultimate wisdom, knowledge and power out there moving everything, animating everything.** God in the third person. Hundreds of billions and billions and billions of years, of light-years.

All of that God in the third-person is now, in this second, sitting in a chair next to you, sitting with you now in this moment, looking at you and desiring you, loving you, knowing every detail of your life, caring about you with infinite tenderness, wanting, your good with full Eros, full tenderness and full power. **Feel that God in the second-person, looking at you, knowing your name and wanting, desiring to hear your prayer.**

I call that *hakadosh baruch hu mit'aveh l'tfilatam shel tzadikim,* **God wants to hear your prayer and wants to meet you, meet me in that prayer.** That is the Infinity of Intimacy. This is the moment to offer up and ask for everything. Friends, this is not a time to be a spectator of all times as the Greeks said, but step in and open our hearts. It is your life! Your dignity, my dignity! We throw ourselves down before the Infinity of Intimacy, and we ask for everything. Lift us like a prayer to the sky, and all prayers are answered, and the word is good, and all obstacles are melted away, *Amen!*

WE CREATE SMALL ISLANDS OF COHERENCE IN A SEA OF SOCIAL CHAOS

Everybody's prayer is coming from the impulse of creation within them, which is the God-force of universal intelligence, creativity, and love itself. Tuning in to the Source from which these prayers are coming, let's all take the prayer that we just prayed and allow it to be infused with the core of the spiral of evolution, going through us, at exactly the frequency of us, carrying that collectively into the universe, into the Reality of who we are. **The Evolutionary Church is the source of intensification of the impulse of creation in every one of us.** We know that *two or more gathered* is greater than us separately. We know that small islands of coherence in a sea of social chaos can shift the actual structure of the universe. Small islands of coherence in a sea of social chaos, which is our world as it is now, can shift the structure of the universe.

What is the structure of the universe that would be shifted?

Here it is: at times of evolutionary crisis, it has been the structure of the universe for billions of years to shift to:

- Higher consciousness
- Greater freedom
- A more complex and loving order

It has shifted from single cell to multi-cell, to animal, to human, to us.

When we pray in the coherent field of a church dedicated to evolutionary planetary love, let us accept the almost unbelievable reality that the force of creation is with us one hundred percent, and that every single prayer that was given is now placed in the field of the planetary shift.

Bruce Lipton is doing a wonderful comedy act coming on as a Jedi with all these funny robes, and he says: *The field is with us!* He said: *It's not the force, it's the field.*

How much coherent field does it take for everybody in that field to be empowered by that field? Let's experiment with that. Let's try that, and let's go down even deeper than our prayer for our specifics. Let's go into our DNA.

I want to read something from an article to you that I have just come across: "New Research Shocks Scientists—Human Emotion Physically Shapes Reality":

> Three different studies done by different teams of scientists prove something really extraordinary: human emotion literally shapes the world around us, not just our perception of the world, but Reality itself.
>
> In the first experiment, human DNA, isolated in a sealed container, was placed near a test object. Scientists gave the donor an emotional stimulus and fascinatingly enough the emotions affected their DNA in the other room.
>
> In the presence of negative emotions, the DNA tightened. In the presence of positive emotions, the coils of the DNA relaxed.
>
> **The scientists concluded human emotion produces effects which defy conventional laws of physics.**
>
> In the second, similar but unrelated experiment, different groups extracted leukocytes, white blood cells from donors and placed them into chambers so they could measure electrical changes in this experiment.
>
> The donor was placed in one room and subjected to emotional stimulus consisting of video clips which generated different emotions to the donor.
>
> The DNA was placed in a different room in the same building.

Both the donor and his DNA were monitored, and as the donor exhibited emotional peaks or valleys, measured by electrical responses, the DNA exhibited the identical responses at the exact same time.[3]

Let's take that seriously. Let's put ourselves in that experiment. Let's take those prayers and feel them emotionally as fulfilled. We take that prayer and see if we can generate the internal emotion that this prayer is being responded to by the process of creation and is being fulfilled now. **Let's place that impulse into the planetary nervous system, the noosphere, the thinking layer of the Earth, and let's surround it with Evolutionary Love.** Coherent love is so powerful. It is drawing from The Universe: A Love Story.

That's our Evolutionary Love code:

The universe is a love story.

Let's take this code, particle to particle all the way up and all the way down, right here and now, as we are experiencing the fulfillment of our prayers. Let's be particles in The Universe: A Love Story here in this church. Let's feel how the particles—that we are—are being attracted to each other. So powerful! Everybody is attracted to everybody else in the field of unconditional love, passionate allurement, intrinsic arousal by evolutionary impulse.

I would like to suggest that—given the tremendous chaos on planet Earth right now, where the fear, dominance, and desire to destroy has been amplified—placing our desire for fulfillment of our prayers into *that field* is essential.

Here is my prayer towards that. It is not so much what Kim Jong Un does or doesn't do or what Donald Trump does or doesn't do. It is about the realization of our purpose.

---

3   Gaelyn Whitley Keith, "New Research Shocks Scientists: Human Emotion Physically Shapes Reality!" TruthWins.com, April 10, 2017, https://truthwins.com/self-talk-blog/67-new-research-shocks-scientists-human-emotion-physically-shapes-reality.

We use this moment of planetary instability to recognize that our purpose is to fill that gap with our love.

It is not only the fulfillment of our personal need and our personal prayers; they go right on up into the gap of a planetary need. **Never before on Earth has there been a greater need for the Church of co-creation,** the Evolutionary Church to co-evolve with nature, co-create with Spirit to bring forth the new human and the new species. Never before has it been so needed.

Our personal prayers, our evolutionary prayers for humanity are now picking up momentum through our deepening of the frequency of that being *so*. In that sense, the prayer power of an Evolutionary Church is more than any of us could possibly do alone.

A MYSTIC IS AN ACTIVIST: LIVING WITH AN UNGUARDED HEART

Let us feel what it is like, my friends, to unguard our hearts. What does it mean to live with an unguarded heart? Reminding us of that set of new neuroscientific information from the article that we just shared, when we speak of emotional structure, it means my heart.

When I unguard, I open up the door, the portal to transformation. I open the door to the Inside of the Inside. I open the door to the Possibility of Possibility.

A person can be giving a sermon in a church with 20,000 people and have a guarded heart. A person can be in the middle of making love and have

31

a guarded heart. Or a person can be mowing the lawn with an unguarded heart. Does everyone feel that?

I invite everyone just to write: *I unguard my heart.*

Am I really willing to say that? Can we write: *I unguard my heart?* Every single one of us? I am not waiting for somebody else to write it and someone else to do it, like, *I am kind of busy; I'll watch how it goes. That would be interesting.* I watch that part which says: *I'm not gonna do this!*

I unguard my heart, every single one of us. When I unguard my heart, I unmute my love. Feel that arising in the world. Pour forth *unguarded!* Feel the space now, everyone, feel into that space. We are that neuroscience experiment. We are it! It is happening right here, just like the children's song: *I open up my heart and let the sun shine in.*

I unguard my heart. What does it feel like to live with an unguarded heart? Wow! **There is room for everything in an unguarded heart.** There is room, it feels open, it feels freedom. What does it feel like? Find the feeling.

Friends, let's take our unguarded heart, and let's infuse. Let's infuse that unguarded heart into the nervous system of the planet. I want to be in deep integrity here. I want to be in deep integrity and bring this into our topic. It is going to jolt you as I say it.

We were in this unguarded heart place, but now we want to be an activist:

- ◆ Let's be social activists.
- ◆ Let's be evolutionary activists.
- ◆ Let's be evolutionary mystics.

Let's remember that *a mystic is an activist.* A mystic is an activist. **As activists, let's pour our unguarded hearts into the noosphere.**

And what is the noosphere? We, like our friend Teilhard de Chardin, describe the noosphere as the nervous system of the planet. Friends, what is the nervous system of the planet today? The nervous system of the planet is the internet. The internet is the nervous system of the planet, and friends, the nervous system of the planet today is not unguarded.

The nervous system of the planet today that connects all of Reality is filled with groups fighting each other. It is filled with a lack of the ability to hear each other. Wael Ghorim, this famous, beautiful man, posted a picture of a man who was murdered by the Egyptian secret police, which began the Arab uprising, known as the Arab Spring some years back. He writes at the beginning of the Arab uprising: *For the liberation of society, we need the internet.* Then on the internet terrible things happened. Smear campaigns and attacks and people crowd-sourced witch hunts against each other; the truth didn't matter, and integrity didn't matter. People posted blog posts about things that didn't happen.

I just read a story[4] this morning about a colonel in the Army who was up for brigadier general and then someone posted a rape story about him from 1986. Only problem was, it wasn't true, and it destroyed his life for four years. That is what is happening, you see? Can you feel, the energy now? All of a sudden, my heart is guarded. Then I think, *Oh my God can I really talk, can I really say, can I really show up? Am I too much? Will I be misinterpreted?* That is why I woke up in the morning scared. I woke up in the morning scared, and I said:

> Marc are you too much? Can you really live as Outrageous Love? Can you really live with your heart open? Maybe you should guard your heart, Marc? Guard your heart. Just go be a professor.

So, I woke up scared this morning. I woke up scared to live with an unguarded heart. **When we live with an unguarded heart, we are so vulnerable.** We are so raw to the world. And everyone wants us to fit into something, but it doesn't work that way.

---

4 See "Jury Orders Blogger to Pay $8.4 Million to Ex-Army Colonel She Accused of Rape," *Washington Post*, August 11, 2017, https://www.washingtonpost.com/news/true-crime/wp/2017/08/11/jury-orders-blogger-to-pay-8-4-million-to-ex-army-colonel-she-accused-of-rape.

We are, all of us together, Jesus. And let us walk together into the Temple. Let's turn over the money tables

Let's turn over that way of living, which is about:

> What can I get from you?
> How can I manipulate you?
> How can I get ahead to feel like I exist when I am so desperately afraid that I don't really exist.

Are we really willing to live with an unguarded heart? Are we willing to be Outrageous Lovers, all of us together? Are we willing to unguard our hearts and say to the internet: *We are going to crowd-source love on the internet?* But not New Age love saying things like: *Okay, I love you; it doesn't matter what you do.*

No, no, we mean love that has deep integrity—Evolutionary Love. Love that brings together. The quarks coming together as three quarks that then form together as hadrons. There are hadrons and muons; they evolve into the first molecules, and molecules become cells. **Can you see the allurement, the Eros, the unguarded heart that causes the dance of love that is Reality?**

When we say together in Evolutionary Church: Reality is a love story, The Universe: A Love Story, we are not making a New Age declaration. We are talking about the deepest nature, scientifically—we are talking about the insights of the interior sciences *and* the exterior sciences—of Reality today. To not know that the universe is a love story is to be insane.

To be insane is to not know the true nature of Reality.

Only a world that *doesn't* realize that the universe is a love story can allow 17,000 children a day to die of hunger or hunger-related diseases, and people with a guarded heart say, *But it is okay because it is not us.* When I can unguard my heart and I feel your joy and pain, we become intimate.

What does it mean to be intimate, my friends? It means, feel me feeling you. That is what it means to be intimate. Intimacy means, feel me feeling you; Feel me feeling you feeling me. Intimacy is not *into-me-you-see.* Intimacy is a feeling in your body. It is a feeling in your body where I feel Barbara-ness, I feel you-ness. I stand for Barbara-ness, I stand for you-ness.

WE MUST CROWD-SOURCE FIERCE OUTRAGEOUS LOVE

In Evolutionary Church we come together not to crowd-source a witch hunt. On the internet today, you can crowd-source a witch hunt. You can create a storyline, you can create a narrative, you can say whatever you want to say. It doesn't matter.

Am I willing to be too much? Am I willing to crowd-source Outrageous Love? That is what the Evolutionary Church is. The response to crowd-sourcing a witch hunt is not to avoid the controversy; it's to walk through it and say *no:*

- We stand in integrity.
- We stand in facts.
- We don't bypass. We don't even bypass the facts.
- We expose untruth.
- We stand fiercely for justice.
- We don't bypass the void; we don't do *a-void-dance.*
- We walk through the void to the other side with Outrageous Love and Outrageous Integrity.

What does it mean when we hold on to our wounds and we say *I am my wound,* and then we exaggerate our wounds beyond imagination, and then we can't climb down the tree because our ego will be fractured? Are we willing to give that up? Are we willing to crowd-source Outrageous Love or does that bore us? Can we crowd-source an Evolutionary Church?

This is our response to crowd-sourcing witch hunts on the internet. This is our response to smear campaigns, our response to the tragedy of our dear friend Donald Trump, who desperately wants to be an Outrageous Lover. The tragedy is not being able to see that.

Oh my God, Donald Trump, we invite you in this moment. Speak fiercely; we want your fierceness and integrity, but we want to feel your goodness. We want to feel your Outrageous Love. Let your Outrageous Love come out, because we know that that's who you are.

We know that every human being desperately wants to live with an unguarded heart, and in Evolutionary Church we are going to model that.

It is our turn. **We are the ones we have been waiting for.** We are the band of Evolutionary Lovers. We are the mystery awake and incarnate in us, and we are not going to do it in a vanilla way. We are not doing vanilla. We are not doing *parve*, as my (Marc's) mother would call it. In Jewish Hebrew *kosher* stuff there are meat dishes and milk dishes and *parve* is in between. My mother would say: *Don't be parve, don't be vanilla*. We are going to be fierce:

- We are going to stand for facts.
- We are going to stand for the evolution of public culture.
- We are going to stand against crowd-sourcing witch-hunts.
- We are going to speak fiercely, and we are going to be on the barricades.
- We are not just going to speak pretty words, dressed up, parading in costumes of New Age. No, we are going to go into the trenches.
- We are going to change the source code in every way.
- We're going to stand against confirmation bias.

- We are going to stand for the innocence of every man and woman, every human being.
- We are going to stand for fair processes, which is what we died for on the beaches of Normandy. For all of it.

But we are going to do it as Outrageous Lovers with unguarded hearts, and even in our fierceness, we are going to keep our hearts open. That is what I woke up scared about in the morning.

BE OUT OF YOUR MIND AND GO INTO YOUR HEART

I bring you my unguarded heart to model that. I woke up scared to be an Outrageous Lover. I woke up scared to live with an unguarded heart. I said:

> Wow it is so scary Marc. Marc, just be a professor, write books, give courses, just do what teachers do. What are you doing? You are out of your mind. I said: Oh my God, I am going to go out of my mind and into my heart!

I want to give you guys a hand motion, as I do it all the time. It is a simple hand motion. You put your hand on your chest, and you just open your heart like a door. You just open your heart, and you say: *I am unguarding my heart.* Try it: I am unguarding my heart. Just try it! I feel where I am going to go out of my mind into my heart and unguard my heart.

That is what we can do. **There are no words—unguarding my heart— no words that can't be spoken.** *I want to know what love is*, and love is Outrageous Love. Love is just putting my hand on the heart and opening. Feel that gesture. It is so powerful. I start as the warrior, pounding my chest, and then I unguard my heart with an opening gesture. With this, right here, right now, you are practicing Outrageous Love. What a powerful gesture! I am unguarding my heart! Yes, I am a warrior. Yes, I am a warrior, pounding, and then I unguard and open my heart.

So, let's hear, let's take that song from Foreigner, and let's not make it foreign, and let's hear the prayers, and let's unguard our hearts. Let's raise it up, let's raise it up and blast it out and let it take us inside. And we take it into activism. *Amen.* "I Want to See What Love Is," Foreigner [See Appendix]

I had a vision and was feeling into the question: *How much coherence does it need to shift the system?* We don't really know the answer to that. We have a hugely incoherent internet system, and my intuition is that the Evolutionary Church is a source code of coherent love, and when we communicate it widely and further, it is what the noosphere requires for the shift of the nervous system of the planet.

We want to take a huge jump like they did in the early church when they believed in the Second Coming of Christ; people did the most heroic things because of that. We believe in the planetary awakening in love. We are doing everything that we can for that, but I want us to put our shared attention on that impulse of unconditional, unguarded love going into our noosphere, so that within the time-frame that we all have to make this shift, we have an Evolutionary Church that reaches the world to contribute to that vision. We are going to have many small Evolutionary Churches rising throughout the planet. We are going to be the source of creation of the DNA of the planet. *Amen.*

We are the revolution; we are the evolution! *Amen!*

CHAPTER THREE

REDEFINING IDENTITY: RESPONDING TO THE TRANSGENDER QUESTION AND RAPE CULTURE WITH EVOLUTIONARY SPIRITUALITY

Episode 43 — August 19, 2017

THE UNIQUE SELF SYMPHONY RESONATES WITH ECSTATIC URGENCY

Because we are the first church to be created to directly express the evolutionary impulse in us internally, socially, politically, and in our species, let the Evolutionary Church pick up the impulse of evolution itself! In resonance, tune in to the impulse of evolution as a vibrational field within you.

It is your unique expression of the 13.8 billion years of genius. **The unique vibration of you coming through you as a member of the Evolutionary Church has an intensification by being recognized as the impulse of the Divine within us, creating us.** Let's celebrate, right here, in this resonant field, the symphony of each of our impulses as a vibrational, even musical, field of expression—the Unique Self Symphony.

What does it feel like if everybody's unique expression begins to resonate in a field far greater than the sum of our parts? **The experience of resonance in the Evolutionary Church is the shared frequencies of the inner impulse within each one of us.**

To hear it, to feel it, and, in this resonant field, to allow the vibrational field to become a symphony this morning.

I just want to share how precious everything is.

I (Marc) just received a text from someone very close to me. Someone whom I had dinner with on Thursday night had a heart attack last night. God willing, they'll be well. I had dinner with this wonderful, world-famous figure. They were my close friend here at the Movement Center. Two stents in their heart.

And the reason I share that now is first because it just happened, and second, it is because the preciousness of it—the preciousness of every moment.

Barbara, I am going to see you this afternoon. How exciting! You are coming to Portland, and we are going to spend a couple of very deep days together envisioning the future of Evolutionary Church and the gorgeous creation and necessity of Evolutionary Church

I just said to myself, as I heard this news, *how precious it is to be in this moment to go in church with my beloved whole mate Barbara,* and to be listening to your voice and resonance and to know that you are coming this afternoon—to know that we have this precious moment, and we are all here in church together.

We think there is something else that needs to happen for us to celebrate; like *if that would happen, we would celebrate.* But the celebration is so intense right now. Rejoicing is so intense right now. It is when we cannot feel the self-evident goodness of life, the self-evident joy—oh my God, that our lives are already a tragedy.

I was talking about you yesterday, Beloved B, to Chetananda,[5] who is very excited to meet you today. I was saying, *Oh my God, Chet, she has more evolutionary vitality than all of us together.*

It is so important to feel into:

- The preciousness of being together
- The preciousness of sharing the impulse together
- The preciousness of creating together
- The preciousness of evolving the source code together
- The preciousness of the holy *Scroll of Esther*
- The preciousness of being

Not only are we in the preciousness of being here right now—the deep quality of being, the eternity that lives in this very moment, the eternity that resides in a moment—but *there is a preciousness and an urgency in now.*

There is a becoming, an evolutionary quality to the depth of being in the now.

There's the ecstatic urgency of becoming which this moment evolves.

We have been talking in Evolutionary Church about evolving public culture. This morning, we are going to be talking about evolving the rape culture, what people mean by rape culture, and what's wrong about that and what's right about that.

But at this time, we are invited to participate in the evolution of love. That is what Evolutionary Church is—the center of everything we believe in. It's our turn. This is the new Bethlehem, and we are on the road to the new Jerusalem.

---

5 Swami Chetananda is an American spiritual teacher of nonduality, particularly Kashmir Shaivism.

Sometimes people say to us, *You guys are getting too excited about this.* Or someone will ask me (Marc), *Why is Barbara so excited?* Or someone will ask Barbara, *Why is Marc being so evangelical about that?*

Because, my friends, this is the good news.

This is the good news, and it is critical.

Our good friend, Zak Stein, our academic director, just came back from a major conference.

And he said that we're at the leading edge, with these memetic structures:

- Unique Self
- Evolutionary Unique Self
- *Homo amor and Homo universalis*
- Conscious Evolution
- Evolutionary Church
- The Universe: A Love Story

We are the leading edge of the leading edge. The invitation in this moment is that Reality needs us to participate in the evolution of love, and it is our turn. **We are the leading edge of the leading edge.**

I know, friends, this is a shocking thing to say, and I wish it was delusional. I wish it was inflation. I wish it was grandiose. It is not.

We are actually holding together an Evolutionary Church, just as they did in da Vinci's circle in the Renaissance and as they did in Bethlehem at the time of the invoking of the New Testament.

We are holding the source code structures of:

- Identity
- Unique Self
- Evolutionary Unique Self
- Awakening a new species
- *Homo universalis*

- A vision of a new universe story

These are utterly essential to bringing us to tomorrow and to confront existential risk.

We are evolution. I am evolution. You are evolution.

We are evolution together,
and it is our turn.

We are willing and ready, God; you invite us, you are demanding that we play a larger game, and we reclaim everything.

We reclaim God at a higher level of consciousness, not the Santa Claus god, but the God who holds us and lives in us, as us, and through us. We reclaim prayer. Not prayer as a slavish obedience to a God with a whip in the sky who demands that we—*No!*

It's prayer—as turning to the Infinity of Intimacy that knows that Barbara is getting on a plane to Portland, and I am picking her up, and that is tracking that event. It's the Infinity of Intimacy that knows our name and that cares and wants to hear Barbara's sermon today—that knows that Barbara and I (Marc) exchanged emails yesterday discussing how we should talk about this today. It's the Infinity of Intimacy that feels everything that is happening.

Imagine that we think about God not merely as the Infinity of Power, but the Infinity of Intimacy. **God in the third person—with billions of light years of power and energy, all the laws of complexity, all the laws of physics, all the power of the universe—is sitting in a chair in front of us.**

God in second-person is knowing everything about us, desiring us, desiring our good, wanting us, and needing our partnership, and loving us so madly that we can bring our holy and our broken *Hallelujahs*—our holy and our broken *Hallelujah* from Lakeland, Connecticut all the way through Jonas

Salk all the way through Colonel Whiteside—the whole thing. The holy and the broken *Hallelujah*, we bring it, we place it before Her, before She. The whole thing.

All of us, we all have it—there is no us and them. We are Evolutionary Church.

We go into prayer, and we bring our holy and broken *Hallelujah*, led by Leonard Cohen, our hymn of Evolutionary Church. "Hallelujah," Leonard Cohen [See Appendix]

And we go now, my friends, like we do every week, and we are laying it down:

> *We are creating the next groove of evolution.*
> *We are creating the next great cosmic habit.*
> *We are creating the next great evolution of love.*

What does prayer mean? Prayer means we go before the Divine, the Infinity of Intimacy, and we ask for everything.

We ask for health.
We ask for friends to recover.
We ask for Barbara to have a safe flight here.
We ask to respond to attacks in public culture with power and grace.
We ask to evolve rape culture.
We ask to have enough money.
We ask for our cancer treatment.

So, let's go in all of us, my friends, and let's begin to pray—*Hallelujah*! We ask for everything.

We don't sit by and watch other people pray. I want to invite you in this moment, step up. When you actually announce it, the prayer, when you speak the words, the great traditions as well as neuroscience tell us that something happens.

As we go in to heal together, to evolve the source code, we are going to dance to an Evolutionary Love song. Let's evolve the source code of culture, the evolutionary impulse as Evolutionary Church. *Amen, amen, amen.*

SETTING THE EVOLUTIONARY CONTEXT: FROM HOMO ERECTUS TO HOMO UNIVERSALIS

What a privilege it is because I can feel in my body, the origin of the impulse of evolution. I can feel the Big Bang, which is continually going forward. I can feel the billions of years it has taken to form the universe, Earth, life, animal life, human life, and now us—at this precise moment of another turn on the evolutionary spiral.

The inner impulse is heating up. **The inner impulse in all of us is awakening and resonating and driving us either to evolutionary extinction or exponential creativity**. We are right between extinction—the misuse of power—and the huge creativity going on exponentially, internally, spiritually, socially, and technologically, leading to the new species.

I want to place the conversation on rape culture in the evolutionary context, so if you don't mind, I'm going to start with *Homo erectus*:

- *Homo erectus* was an amazing creature, but pretty much a scavenger. It hardly ate meat. It was scavenging. Imagine, with no language, just herbs, grasses and the animals, doing its best for millions of years.
- Then came *Homo neanderthalensis*, who were evidently quite intelligent—burying food with their dead—but was not much of a hunter either—mainly still eating vegetation and small animals.
- And then folks, in came *Homo sapiens*. *Homo sapiens* arrived on the scene—the greatest killer that there ever was. This genius species was capable, for the very first time, of developing the tools to kill the very large animals.

If we can, imagine the scene of these early *Homo sapiens* gaining the materials to go after buffalo and huge animals, going after them and winning over them, then having understanding of fire and being able to cook these meats, and being able to wipe out *Homo erectus* and *Homo neanderthal*, as well as most of the large animals.

Then as we traveled across the globe, we had to deal with whatever the weather was, and we did.

I was reading an important book called *After Eden: The Evolution of Human Domination.*[6] According to the author, after the period of *Homo sapiens* prevailing, we were heading, and are heading, toward ecocide, the destruction of the entire environment by our enormous capacity to prevail, to kill, to win, and to eat.

We are also heading toward geocide because on the one hand, it is the environment, and on the other hand, let's say we start with nuclear weapons. That is what started me (Barbara) in all of this, in 1945—the fact that we can destroy the whole world many times over with the bombs we already have, and those in power think they should have more. Sapiens still, to some degree, are prevailing in this situation of the vast escalation of power, very near global destruction and an exponential jump.

This is why the Evolutionary Church is so important. Because what other organization, entity, or set of ideas comes in at the exact moment of this evolutionary shift that is greater than between *Homo erectus*, *Homo Neanderthal*, and *Homo sapiens*? Right now, this evolutionary shift is between *Homo sapiens* either pursuing our capacity to destroy and destroy everything or creating something new.

Something new is in our church. How did we get from *Homo sapiens* to this next stage of evolution? What happened there?

---

6 Kirkpatrick Sale, *After Eden: The Evolution of Human Domination* (Durham, NC: Duke University Press, 2006).

Without taking any time for any historical thing, we do want to say something as simple as the sentence: *All men are created equal.*

The declaration of human rights, democracy, that everybody counts is a huge, amazing step forward. Within that, the individual rights of women, who were always underneath the thumb of the men and needed to be because they needed to be protected in the world of *Homo sapiens.* So women arose.

Born in 1929, I (Barbara) grew up as one of those early women who, in the 1960s, married, had as many babies as possible, loved your husband, took care of your house, and learned to cook.

This woman you see before you now did all of that for almost 20 years. I was not a rebel; I was really trying to do what I was told. And finally, I got deeply depressed.

Then I discovered Maslow, who said that chosen work makes you self-actualizing, and then I discovered my chosen work. Now you see me in front of you as an evolutionary woman, and I am one of the earliest versions of what millions of us are now becoming as women. But because of the anger that has built up in women, some women are misinterpreting men and declaring they are being raped—calling it rape culture.

We have also seen the evolution of Black Lives Matter. We have seen the anger among transgender people against those who aren't accepting them. It is a sea of anger.

But what really is the direction of the sea of anger and creativity that we are heading toward, as *Homo sapiens* could destroy everything through ecocide and geocide? **We are angry with each other, and our democracies are failing us because they are win/lose democracies.**

I believe in the purpose of the Evolutionary Church, right in the midst of that, between the destruction of our species and the evolution. I am going to call us *Homo universalis.*

Another book I was reading this morning was called *Homo Deus*[7] by Yuval Harari.

I just returned from Singularity University,[8] where I met a lot of high-tech geniuses. According to the beautiful book *Homo Deus*—which is really fun and interesting—humans are now working toward three basic things: to be like gods, to be immortal, and to be in a state of bliss.

The next stage of human evolution, according to where our culture is heading: Google has hired Ray Kurzweil's colleague, Arthur Levinson, *to solve death.*

This means we are evolving beyond the animal-human condition here. One way or the other, *Homo sapiens* has completed its journey and is giving birth to a new species, right now. **I think we have to weigh in on what kind of species it should be because it is going to make the entire difference for all the rest of history.**

I believe *Homo universalis* is at this very deep choice point that will deal with things like rape culture, the accusation of one another, and the destruction of each other as has been the negative part of our strength and our greatness.

And at this choice-point we are nurturing the qualities for the next stage— to deal with rape culture and all the other violence in the world. The first of it is the evolution of spirituality itself. Or even before that, the universe is a love story—re-visioning of the story of evolution itself, from the origin of creation, quark with quark, electron with electron, proton with proton... all the way on up—allurement and attraction at the core of creation.

Homo universalis is aware of that historically and feels it. That is why we are a church of Evolutionary Love. We feel that enormity of attraction.

---

7 Yuval Noah Harari, *Homo Deus: A Brief History of Tomorrow* (New York: Harper, 2017)

8 Singularity University, founded by futurists Ray Kurzweil and Peter Diamandis, is an educational organization that equips leaders with knowledge of advanced technologies to address global challenges and drive innovation.

Now here we are, waking up in the midst of geocide, ecocide, or evolution, and we are feeling that love. The first quality is the internal spirituality we feel, which is different from just feeling *a God from on high.*

We feel the impulse of evolution going through billions and billions of years of learning of how to evolve into our own inner experience, of evolutionary spirituality—which is a book that Marc and I are working on.

THE MEANING OF OUR NEW POWER: INCARNATING AS CO-CREATORS WITH THE DIVINE

Evolutionary spirituality is the spirituality of the genius of evolution, incarnate as our impulse to evolve. **Evolutionary spirituality is the incarnation of evolution's 13.8-billion-year genius in creating an entire universe, now incarnating as our spiritual contact with the Divine.**

The Divine is seen as the operating principle of creation itself in us as we become co-creators. This is being cultivated now in the Evolutionary Church, and *Homo universalis* is incarnating the spirit of love as co-creators.

How does that come to us socially? *Homo universalis* is vocationally aroused. Have you noticed I am vocationally aroused? But what is vocation? It is the calling of evolution from within you.

Reality needs you, not just us, but you, me, each one of us.

Reality needs us to express unique creativity such that the divine genius of evolution is coming right through us, and we are becoming an impulse of creation itself—vocationally.

That is the way I believe we feel in the Evolutionary Church.

I personally feel that the goal of a planetary awakening with a Unique Self Symphony and all the subsystems that need to happen before that can happen is my goal.

What is your goal? We did not even dare to have goals like that before. I remember people saying to me, *You think you're having an effect on evolution? You must be crazy.* Of course, I think that because I *am* having an effect on evolution.

So, **my vocation has a spirituality that is combining evolution, life purpose, work in the world, and creativity**—all of that is in *Homo universalis* and is being inspired personally, every one of us. Then we want to add to that the tremendous genius of high technology.

How come our species has been given the power of our ancient gods? What happened here?

For me, it started when we dropped the atomic bombs on Japan, and I asked the question then that guided my life: *What is the meaning of our new power that is good?* What are the images of the future that are equal to the power that is good? I (Barbara) was fifteen years old then, so I started to ask people, and I found that nobody knew.

Not only did they not know, but they had also never asked. And my most fun story here, of course, is asking this of President Eisenhower in 1953. I got into the Oval Office and said, Mr. President, I have a question for you: *What do you think the meaning is of all this new power, military, industrial, technological, scientific power that is good?*

Eisenhower looked at me, shook his head, and said, *I have no idea.* I replied, *Well, Mr. President, we'd better find out.*

Between 1953, when I met the president, and 2017, I think we found the answer.

The meaning of our new power is a new species, capable of co-creating with the Divine—a new species we are calling *Homo universalis*, which is an expression of divine love.

50

Then we add:

- Nanotech
- Biotech
- Quantum computing
- Global intelligence
- Genetics

Then we pick up the impulse of love with the impulse of creativity and vocation, and we find our part in using those high technologies for the greater transformation of humanity—how do we feel then? Vocationally aroused, I can tell you that.

The next thing is that we have to find partners. There is absolutely no way that anybody does this alone.

One of the great things about being a member of the Evolutionary Church is that we are partners in the deepest and highest sense.

We are partnering with the collective creative impulse that resides in each of us.

Now, it is enough to have it inside yourself and to say *yes* to yourself—individually *yes, I am going to do whatever it is I am called to*. But what if we join with two, three, four, fifty, a hundred thousand—what then?

So, we take this and go into the noosphere, into the global intelligence system, into the mass media, into social media, and we state: *Our crisis is the birth of a universal, co-creative humanity, and everybody is needed.*

If we consider rape culture in the midst of all that, it loses its interest because all the people concerned about that, the women who are concerned about being raped by men or men who are perhaps even still dominating women, will disappear—just like *Homo erectus* and *Homo neanderthal* and early *Homo sapiens* are gone.

WE DO NOT LIVE IN A RAPE CULTURE; WE LIVE IN A LOVE CULTURE

There are those who cry out against the darkness, and there are those who add light.

Of course, we have to cry out against the darkness, and of course, we stand a billion percent against any form of rape:

- Millions of men being raped in prisons.
- Women being raped in third-world countries.
- Whatever tragedy of rape lives in America.

But rape is not a man-woman issue.

The problem with the phrase *rape culture,* first, is that it is not true. It's not true in the sense that, looking at the literature, it casts men as predators and women as victims. It says that the nature of our culture is a rape culture. Well, that is not actually true. **Our culture is a culture of love.**

Our culture is a culture where people are doing a billion gorgeous things every second to help each other and hold each other:

- Parents raising children
- People loving each other
- People creating for each other
- People looking to stand for each other
- People dying for each other
- People sacrificing for each other
- People meeting each other's eyes
- People holding hands

We have tragedy when we define rape culture by making it only due to men, by making that all of culture and where we put our obsessed energy— instead of talking about all the people who suffer from it.

Of course, we stand against rape. We stand against any man who is raped in prison, any woman who is raped in prison, or any man or woman who is raped anywhere.

We stand against murder. We stand against torture. We do not live in a *torture culture*. We live in a *love culture*. We live in The Universe: A Love Story.

The reason we are horrified by rape, the reason we are horrified by murder, is because murder and rape are tragic *failures of intimacy*.

And the reason we are horrified by the tragic failures of intimacy is because the world is not merely a materialist chance and random world. **The best evolutionary science, the best complexity theory, the best chaos theory, and the best interior sciences of all the great traditions tell us that the universe is a love story.**

I know in my body, first person, that it's true—that evolution is true, and that evolution means the universe is not just an eternal love story, the universe is an Evolutionary Love Story.

> *It means that Reality is not a fact; it is a story.*
> *It is not an ordinary story.*
> *It is a love story.*
> *It is not an ordinary love story.*
> *It is an Evolutionary Love story.*
> *It is an Outrageous Love story.*

And the story is of moving from *Homo neanderthalensis* and *Homo erectus* to *Homo sapiens*, and to ultimately moving to *Homo imaginus*. The human being is Adam. Adam in Hebrew means "imagine." Adam includes in the original biblical text both Adam and Eve. We are *Homo imaginus*. We are re-imagining.

And the crisis we face today, at its core, is a crisis of imagination. We need to re-imagine Reality—that's what we've just done so beautifully.

Let's join in that imagination. *Let's reset the very source code of culture itself with this new vision of identity with Homo imaginus, with the Unique Self, and Evolutionary Unique Self.*

This is that moment in Evolutionary Church when we restate the entire story.

We do not live in a rape culture. We have to deal with rape that hurts men and women. We have to stop demonizing men and making women into victims.

- Both men and women are gorgeous expressions of evolution.
- Both men and women have great light and potential shadow.
- Both men and women need to evolve beyond their shadow into the gorgeous unique expressions of light that they are.

Whenever people demonize men, I think about the opening scenes from that movie with Tom Hanks many years ago, called *Saving Private Ryan*. It was an incredible movie. The scene was men pouring out of the ships on the beaches of Normandy, hundreds of thousands of men, knowing that so many of them would be killed. Yet they pour out of those boats, put their lives on the line, and sacrificed their lives so that we can be here today in Evolutionary Church.

And most of the death professions, the dangerous professions that keep the world moving today, 96% are men. Do you know that men die on average eight years earlier than women? Imagine if it was reversed and women died eight years earlier than men. We would have the entire country up in arms. But it is okay with everyone that the suicide rate for boys, when they start having to perform the male role around fifteen or sixteen, is four times that of girls.

The demonization of men has to stop. We have to love men and love women in full beauty and know who we are. **This is where the transgender movement is so totally right in their question, but wrong in the response.**

UNIQUE GENDER: A BETTER RESPONSE TO THE TRANSGENDER QUESTION OF WHO AM I?

What is the transgender movement saying?

There is something deeper than *man* that I am, and something deeper than *woman*. I sense that I'm not just a girl or a boy; those terms don't define me. There's something deeper. Who am I?

But they do not have an answer. It's not just that I am a unique combination of men and women. They don't quite know how to answer it.

It is not just what we talk about. We have a very major idea that is coming down that we are all a unique gender.

Unique gender means that we are unique combinations of the masculine and feminine, which are unique expressions of the evolutionary impulse.

But it is even deeper than that. The transgender movement is saying, *I want a deeper identity. I know I am deeper than that. I know I am more than just boy or girl. Who am I?*

I am evolution. That is the deeper answer. I am. I know the answer to the question of *who are you?*

The new credo of *Homo universalis* that we're bringing down into the world is:

> *You are an irreducibly unique expression of the LoveIntelligence and LoveBeauty that is the initiating and animating Eros and energy of All-That-Is,*
> *that lives in you, as you, and through you, that never was, is, or will be ever again—other than through you. And as such,*

we stand on the abyss of darkness, and we can say, let there be
light. Let there be a unique singularity of light that never was,
is, or will be ever again.

The singularity is you.

You are the singularity.

You are ontologically orthogonal to anything that's come before you.

What does orthogonal mean? It means a right-angle, meaning there is nothing like you that ever was before. You are the singularity. **You are an irreducibly unique expression of the LoveIntelligence and LoveBeauty that is the initiating and animating Eros and energy of All-That-Is, that lives in you, as you, and through you.**

And you awaken as *Homo universalis;* you awaken as Unique Self, and when you claim that identity, when you know that as such, there is a unique need.

There is a unique need within your circle of intimacy and influence that can be realized and met by your gifts alone. As such, you have a unique set of gifts—emerging from your unique perspective and quality of intimacy— which give you the capacity to address this need as no one else ever could; not in the past, present, or future.

When we realize that, we can declare with confidence:

> *I am evolution.*
> *I am the personal face of the evolutionary impulse.*
> *I am the personal essence of the evolutionary impulse awakened*
> *as each one of us.*
> *That evolution lives in me, as me, and through me.*
> *And that evolution, now here's the deepest Inside of the Inside,*
> *evolution is not merely a process, it is an intimate process.*

The Universe feels, and the Universe feels love. **Love's not hard to find. Love is impossible to avoid. Love animates and suffuses Reality in every second.**

We do not live in a rape culture—we live in a love culture. And it is not a love culture in a New Age way. It is not pretty words parading around in costumes.

Sometimes, as Hafiz writes in one of his great poems, "A Barroom View of Love,"[9] *sometimes love hurts so much*, he says, *it is like taking hold of the swollen balls of an elephant holding on to you, gripping you hard, and not having the good fortune to die.*

Love is sometimes painful. We are not talking about love with a small *L*. We are talking about Evolutionary Love. We are talking about knowing that the allurement that drives quarks, electrons, and protons dances in us, and that we—you—are needed by All-That-Is.

All-That-Is waits—All-That-Is waits—for Maria Bell[10] to arise and bring forth and proclaim liberty throughout the land. The Liberty Bell is each of us, entering and transforming the source code, as us vocationally arousing The Universe: A Love Story.

It is us.

In every generation, at the leading edge, there is a group of people who, for whatever reason, are somehow awakened—not better than anyone else. They are a global communion of inspired souls who know the wheel of creation, the Wheel of Co-creation 2.0, the new map, the new vision of identity, the new Universe Story.

---

9   "A Barroom View of Love" is a poem by the fourteenth-century Persian poet Hafiz, renowned for his mystical and ecstatic verses. This particular poem has been translated and interpreted by various scholars and poets.

10   Maria Bell follows the tradition of naming significant bells after "Maria" or "Mary" as a nod to the religious or reverential status these bells held. The Liberty Bell is inscribed with the Bible verse, "Proclaim LIBERTY Throughout all the Land unto all the Inhabitants Thereof" (Lev. 25:5–10).

Friends, this is not about commodifying our message to sell it back to the masses—no one owns it. It belongs to all of us, and it is ours to bring to life together. This is about shifting our perspective from *I* to *we*; it's about beginning to speak with a collective voice.

It is not just about joining genes, it is about joining genius. It is about knowing that we can do this together; that Evolutionary Church needs to be not just the gorgeous, beautiful, stunning, and deep devotion of five thousand people who have joined from all over the world, but it has to be five-thousand, five hundred thousand, a million. When I say five million, some would say that was a fantasy. No! Fifty million.

And when I say fifty million, if you say, *wow, that is fantasy*. No, fifty million is not enough—500 million. We have to be a billion rising.

My friends, the noosphere—the nervous system of the planet—is the internet. And as the great Broadway play *Avenue Q* says, *the internet is for porn*. That is bad erotica. What about Eros? What about the internet that connects The Universe: A Love Story?

What about knowing that the noosphere is precious like my friend who just had a heart attack? My friend had a heart attack. Reality is having a heart attack. The heart is being attacked. Let's sit in our hearts and know that our hearts are not just egocentric, not just ethnocentric, not even just worldcentric for the sake of all humanity, but that we are cosmocentric expressions of Evolutionary Love. We are evolution.

LET'S GO FROM D-DAY TO E-DAY: WE ARE EVOLUTION

We are evolution. We proclaim this together! Can you feel that?

We are, I am, we are evolution.

Let's proclaim it.

Let's declare it.

We are evolution.

The whole world is in our hands. We can fix the whole thing. We are evolution. Let's hear it rise up. Let the Liberty Bell ring to the land. But let's not be embarrassed to be evangelicals. Are we excited? Yes, we are excited:

- We are excited because Barbara is evolution.
- We are excited because Marc is evolution.
- We are excited because Lisa is evolution,
- And because we are daring enough not to say I, but to say *we are evolution.*

Barbara spoke to President Eisenhower and asked, *what is the meaning of our power?* We are now articulating for the first time together—joining memes—the best answer available in the world to that question, and we are standing for it together: **we are evolution.**

We are in all the mechanizations behind the scenes, all the political intrigues, and all the energy of destruction. We are going to transform it into the energy of creation. We are evolution.

We have the whole world. We can make the whole thing happen. We are evolution.

When I (Barbara) saw the movie *D-Day* a while ago, I had a dream that night that Eisenhower came to me and said, *Barbara, call for E-Day.* I interpreted that to mean *evolution day* or *emergence day.*

So I'm calling for E-Day: Ecstatic, Emergence, Evolutionary Day. Eureka! *Eureka Day.*

What would that be like if you say all those brave men walked into the field of the Nazis being shot at? But for us, for freedom, we have been given this. Thank you, God. Thank you, brave people that did this. Thank you, Eisenhower and De Gaulle and Churchill and everybody who fought the Nazis.

Our next step is E-Day. **Everybody who feels this everywhere, let's dedicate ourselves to E-Day. As church, the Evolutionary Church, let's dedicate to E-Day.**

When we give to the E-Church, Evolutionary Church, we are giving to humanity right now but building toward a radical transformation. I believe it will be the awakening of a new species.

E-Day it is.

I would love to have everybody who hears about it go and celebrate E-Day wherever they are, like the troops headed there towards being killed on behalf of freedom. Wow.

Okay, everybody. E-Day it is. E-Day is here. Today is the first E-Day because we have declared it to be so: Ecstatic, Eros, Eureka, Evolution, Emergence, E-Day. *Amen.*

CHAPTER FOUR

AN EVOLUTIONARY CHURCH COLLECTIVE IS A SYMPHONY OF UNIQUE EXPRESSIONS OF LOVEINTELLIGENCE

Episode 45 — September 2, 2017

RESONATING AS MEMBERS OF THE FIRST EVOLUTIONARY COLLECTIVE

Here is this week's Evolutionary Love code:

> I am a Unique Self. I am an irreducibly unique expression of the LoveIntelligence and LoveBeauty that is the initiating and animating Eros of All-That-Is that lives in me, as me, and through me, that never was, is, or will be ever again, other than through me.

All right, everybody, I (Barbara) am speaking from Zurich, and in Zurich there are many people who are *Homo universalis*. They are everywhere around Zurich. They did not know that they were here until I arrived. And **it is really nice to be able to give people a sense of a name and the species that they are becoming.** In light of that, let's feel this resonance today, as it brings us into the experience of being a member of an Evolutionary Church collective.

The word *member* is very deep. It does not mean just that I am part of your organization; **being a member means that I am a *living* member of the very first evolutionary collective, dedicated to the planetary awakening in love**. The only thing I really can relate to in the form of churches that have been formed in the past is the early Christian church that was dedicated in the love of Christ, to the second coming; in the words of Pierre Teilhard de Chardin, *an awakening of love on the planet.*

Those early members believed this was possible, even though the church lost its way when it was taken over by emperors and powers—largely because it was so powerful. We will not let this happen to us. To become a member of an evolutionary collective dedicated to planetary awakening is to connect with the very power of Earth."

Those early Christians completely changed the world. The pioneering women who advanced women's rights changed the world. And early people of color who demanded equality after slavery changed the world.

We stand in this tradition, pausing to resonate for a moment, as an evolutionary collective of emerging humans. We feel our presence expanding across the Earth, rising up at this critical juncture of planetary challenge—amid missed growth and misused power—to become co-creators of a conscious, loving planetary evolution.

Becoming an evolutionary collective for the purpose of the planetary awakening gives a certain weight to the pivot point on planet Earth, which we could think of as a very delicate balance between devolution and Conscious Evolution.

What is the key to shifting it in the direction of a positive future?

Let's assume that an evolutionary spiritual collective, dedicated to the planetary awakening through the Unique Self Symphony, is a factor in the positive future of the next stage of evolution. Feel yourself participating in an awesome generation of new potential to your unique attraction to being together. Thank you, thank you God.

PRAYER BEYOND SEPARATION: PRAYING AS UNIQUE SELVES

Beloved Barbara from Zurich. I (Marc) have been getting fabulous reports from Zurich regularly and have received at least two reports daily, so I have a good sense of it. They had an awesome event in Zurich about people becoming *Homo universalis*. It is the moment we are talking about, becoming members of the new species. But, first let's just clarify.

We are just getting ready for prayer:

- We are all here.
- We can all see each other.
- We are all present.
- We are not just at another event.
- It is not something on our schedule, *oh, we have church in between this and in between that.*

We are at the great convening this morning. This is the great convening in this generation.

Can you imagine? They must have felt this in Bethlehem: Hey, my wife needs me home, or My husband needs me, We have the neighbor to deal with, We have to fix something, The blacksmith needs me—in other words, all the normal pressures of life were there then, as they are now. But something momentous was happening. **To be aware that something momentous is happening when it is happening is what it means to be an awakened human being**.

We are in this week of convening membership as Unique Selves, and the way we understand, it is our identity. We're not going to talk about that yet; I wanted to create the relationship so it is clear. We are each Unique Selves, and that means We are Unique Selves all of us together, members of the new species of *Homo universalis*.

Unique Self and *Homo universalis* are not the same thing

Unique Selves are individual members of the species of Homo universalis.

That is a Unique Self.

And as we move into prayer, let's get it straight: uniqueness invites and implies prayer. If I'm just a separate self, destined to die, and death is the end of the story, that I'm obliterated, and my life is, as Hobbes said, *nasty, brutish, and short*—then prayer becomes the old prayer.

The old prayer is, *make it a little less painful, and let's have a little more glory while we are here. We pray to the cosmic vending machine in the sky that our religion happens to own, to make sure that we get a new car, and we stay healthy.* While these are legitimate goods, they are not really what we mean by prayer.

We are in church—evolving God.

We are evolving prayer as God asks us to do.

When we talk about prayer, we mean something else. We do not mean that we are all part of the One, so just forget about what you need and just merge into the One, be part of the One—if that were the case, then of course you wouldn't ask for your needs. Only separate selves would do that.

We are going to blow the roof open right now. Unique Self actually is what prayer is about.

The new vision of prayer, the evolution of prayer, the reclaiming of prayer, is directly dependent on realizing that we are not a separate self. We are not just separate from All-That-Is—*life is nasty, brutish, and short*, so let me pray for what I can get as best as I can. That is not an accurate view of identity. That is a lie.

And I am not only a True Self—just part of the One. The total number of True Selves is one, and if I'm just part of the One, then why would I ask for anything for me, because I'm just part of the One?

There is no true prayer as a separate self the way we are going to talk about prayer. And there is no true prayer as merely True Self or merely part of the one.

Only as a Unique Self do we pray, because—as a Unique Self—we realize our stories matter: our stories are chapters in the cosmic scroll, the largest story of all.

But our stories do not disappear into the One. Our stories are *unique expressions of the One*, and our needs matter, not merely as our personal needs, but our needs are the needs of the One; they are the unique needs of the One expressed in me. The entire One, the entire cosmic scroll, needs the letter in that cosmic scroll whose name is *me,* the letter whose name is *you.* The entire Cosmic scroll prays for your needs to be detailed. Your needs are fulfilled not only for you but for Reality having a you experience.

When Barbara prays for her needs, when Marc prays for his needs, when we pray for our needs, not merely as a small separate self, grasping, but as a unique expression of the seamless coat of the universe, the entire seamless coat of the universe, the entire one All-That-Is, responds. Prayer affirms the dignity of personal need by recognizing that our individual needs reflect the infinite dignity of our Unique Self—not as a separate entity, but as an interconnected expression of being.

My Unique Self is part of the greater fabric of the One, is needed by All-That-Is, and is inseparable from All-That-Is. It is only if:

> My needs are fulfilled,
> My Eros is alive,
> I am awake,
> I am pulsating,
> I am delighted, and

I am radically alive…

…that I can I give my gift into the whole that the whole desperately needs.

The context for prayer is our first code. This is what we mean by evolving the source code. It's not just another little moment we have on our schedule. **We are evolving the source code, realizing that to evolve prayer we need to evolve our identity**.

Only Unique Selves can pray in the way that prayer really means, asking for everything—for every personal need, knowing that all those needs are needed, not just by me, but they are needed by All-That-Is.

And if our friends Rhoda and Shimmer are in a hospital this weekend, with Rhoda taking care of Shimmer, and the hospital does not have electricity and is powered by a generator, Oh my God.

We are with each other, right now, in every way. **We are not separate; each of your needs, my needs, are our needs.** Thousands of us are gathered from all over the world, and we are going to ask for everything. We offer up our prayers before the Divine, the Infinity of Intimacy that both lives in us and holds us in every second—the Infinity of Intimacy that knows our name. We offer up our holy and our broken *Hallelujah* as Unique Selves, members of the new species *Homo amor*. No one is left out.

We are not spectators. All of us are in the Inside of the Inside, together.

Let's feel the prayers, and let them rise up:

- Prayer rises on our enthusiasm.
- Prayer rises on our ecstasy.
- Prayer rises on our rapture.

The sacred texts say that if there is no healer, if there is no awesomeness, and if there is no Outrageous Love, the prayer does not rise.

There's a beautiful story that Martin Buber tells about the *Baal Shem Tov*:

The *Baal Shem Tov* goes to a synagogue. It's a very large synagogue, and there are only a few people who have come there to pray. They ask him to come and give a lecture there.

Baal Shem Tov: *I cannot go into the synagogue.*

People: *Why can't you go into the synagogue?*

Baal Shem Tov: *Because there is no room in there for me.*

People: *What do you mean there is no room? There's only 30 people there, and there is room for 170.*

Baal Shem Tov: *There is no room there because none of the prayers have risen. Because when the prayers do not have rapture, and they do not have ecstasy, and they do not have enthusiasm, and people aren't with us and witnessing each other's prayers, then the prayer cannot rise.*

Let them rise.

We are afraid of rapture and are so locked in our egoic structures that we cannot quite feel someone else's prayer.

We have to feel everyone's prayer, to feel it in our hearts as these prayers are lifting up and rising to the sky.

Prayers only lift up when we have signed our Unique Self on the prayer, and that is the secret of prayer—**prayer and Unique Self are intimately related**.

If I don't sign my Unique Self on my prayer, my unique rapture, my unique ecstasy, my unique vulnerability—the prayer cannot rise.

May those prayers rise to the sky, and we are now going to catch a ride on those prayers with our next message, and lift us up into the next heaven as we open up the first code of Evolutionary Church here in Bethlehem all over the world.

THE UNIQUE SELF CREDO: THE FIRST CODE EVOLUTIONARY CHURCH

It's a great privilege today to bring forth this first code. This is one of the great, deep understandings upon which the entire movement is based.

> You are an irreducibly unique expression of the LoveIntelligence and LoveBeauty that is the initiating and animating Eros love of All-That-Is that lives in us, through us, and as us.

Let's take it phrase by phrase.

You are a Unique Self. This is totally stunning. First of all, everything in the universe is unique. We've heard that every snowflake, and whatever Divine Intelligence is up to—everything—is unique.

God could have created a robotic universe where everything was created by God and run through that God Force, but it would have been a universe without freedom.

Suppose we took that freedom out of all the snowflakes, cells, and all the galaxies of the universe, except this little planet Earth with you being unique—we're still left with the deep preciousness of everything within us, and that which impels us to express our uniqueness.

Then if I focus my attention on what is motivating me and you and all of us to express our uniqueness. It really is the impulse of evolution. It really is the impulse of creation. **It really is the God Force that's providing us the opportunity to be original for the sake of God.**

The awesome blessing of being unique in an entire universe of life!

You Are an Irreducibly Unique Expression of the LoveIntelligence. Irreducibly.

---

*We cannot be reduced to anything
less than this whole uniqueness
that we intrinsically are.*

We can never see ourselves as simply a particle, a person in a universe without freedom. We will recognize the importance of this idea for democracy as we continue.

Let's start with the LoveIntelligence that is animating the universe. Have you ever considered the awesome nature of the LoveIntelligence animating the universe?

It is uniquely in each one of us. It's overwhelmingly intelligent:

> Every quark,
> every electron,
> every proton,
> every single cell,
> every multi-cell,
> all these billions and billions of unique cells,
> all of that DNA that makes all these eyes and ears and thumbs...

You and I are unique expressions of the awesome intelligence that expresses uniquely as us.

Being a Unique Self does not mean we each have to do *everything*—it means we have to do *only the things that are uniquely ours to do.*

It is absolutely essential that as we feel the unique LoveIntelligence, we discover how to express it. It's not enough for me to be the unique LoveIntelligence of the universe and just sit on it. It really isn't. Those of us who say *Yes* to the impulse of evolution are saying *Yes* to that unique impulse in us with the intelligence of the Universe.

Here's a discovery of what happens if we say *Yes* to it, realizing it is the LoveIntelligence of the universe and not just of us individually: *you get more intelligent.*

That's what happens. We are drawing on the LoveIntelligence of the universe as us uniquely, able to express itself through us. It is our heart's desire, our yearning, our longing for more love, more life, more beauty, more expression of who we are. It's the force of nature itself in you.

Sometimes people say to me (Barbara), *Well, you know, you can do that, but I'm just a housewife, and I couldn't do what you're doing.*

I answer: *I was a housewife with five children, and I was depressed. I could understand it, but it wasn't because I was a housewife that I couldn't do this.*

Finally, what happened was I realized (through Abraham Maslow, Pierre Teilhard de Chardin, Ken Wilber, Marc, and my own discoveries) who this particular person that I am, you are, is not only uniquely expressing the intelligence but is impelled to discover whatever is intelligent about each of our uniqueness.

For everyone who's praying for everything, let's also pray for the unique intelligence—LoveIntelligence—to come out the whole way.

Sometimes I let myself go when somebody asks, *What is it that the unique LoveIntelligence wants within you?* I dare to take the lid off the top of my prayer, the lid off the top of my life, and answer, *the LoveIntelligence within me that comes from the entire story of creation uniquely as me has given me a unique function to play in my most deep attraction, which is the planetary awakening.*

Then I feel that my vocation, the thing that I am doing right here, talking with you in the Evolutionary Church is supremely important, instead of thinking, *well, what difference could I make?* I am the LoveIntelligence of the universe uniquely doing this. If I am left out, then expressing the LoveIntelligence and LoveBeauty that is the initiating and animating Eros of All-That-Is is left out.

Now, consider the LoveBeauty that is initiating and animating All-That-Is. **Have you noticed that everything that endures is beautiful?** It is really amazing.

Think about it, that in our particular globe and world:

- Every bird
- Every fish
- Every snake
- Every spider
- Every worm

Everything that endures and exists for any length of time is beautiful.

Let's just take a horse. If we look at the Eohippus—the early horse—it was awkward, but as it matured it got more and more beautiful until we see these sleek and beautiful animals today.

Or take *Homo erectus, Homo neanderthalensis,* and *Homo sapiens*—pretty awkward-looking many of them, but then let's take *Venus de Milo.* Let's take the most beautiful person that we have ever seen and see that the trajectory of evolution is toward more beauty.

> *Everything that endures is beautiful, or it goes extinct.*

That's why, when we look out at nature it's glorious. That is the same for us.

If we continue to evolve, we are going to be ever more beautiful, and everything that we create that endures is going to be ever more beautiful— the initiated animal. I am the LoveIntelligence that is initiating—making it work.

We have to be an initiator. We cannot sit on this and say somebody else is going to do it. **Initiating and animating Eros, we are animated by the love of the Universe.**

You are animated. *The church* is animated by a collective love of all the people who know *they* are animated by the love of the Universe.

What is going to happen to this church? A church of Evolutionary Love has not ever been able to exist at such a time of planetary birth—ever! *Never!*

Let's take this as a collective: that everybody in this collective is a tiny microcosm. It never shows up at the top of the Empire State Building. They are all small to begin with, and we feel in ourselves, as a collective Evolutionary Church, that we are holding this Code for everybody.

If we can manifest this as individuals, as a collective of individuals, and as a church, and express it in various ways throughout the world, just as I (Barbara) am doing here in Zurich, who knows how much can grow from us?

I was thinking because we all have this love of democracy that we might expand Thomas Jefferson's words to say: *all people are created uniquely endowed by our Creator to express our uniqueness for the good of the self and the whole.*

We are evolving our culture by doing this. We are evolving the next stage of democracy by doing this. We believe we are evolving the next stage of everybody's life when we say *yes* to *You are a unique.*

Let's be irreducibly gorgeous and unique.

MY UNIQUE SELF IS IN DEVOTION TO SOMEONE ELSE'S UNIQUE SELF

We are ready to state, restate, state again, and live our first code:

I am a Unique Self.

I am an irreducibly unique expression of the LoveIntelligence and LoveBeauty that is the initiating and animating Eros of All-That-Is that lives in me, as me, and through me, that never was, is, or will be ever again, other than through me.

I am a unique expression of Evolutionary Love.

I am a unique expression of the LoveIntelligence that is the initiating and animating Eros of All-That-Is.

What is that? That is Evolutionary Love; that is Outrageous Love.

To say, *I am a Unique Self* is to say, *I am a unique Outrageous Lover*—not ordinary love, not the strategy of the ego of the separate self. I want you to get how deep the code is.

Ordinary love is what we do to get comfort and security which is a strategy of the separate self. Outrageous Love, Evolutionary Love, that's an expression of Unique Self.

We can only say—*I am an Outrageous Lover; we live in a world of outrageous pain; the only response to outrageous pain is Outrageous Love*—as a Unique Self.

Only a Unique Self can be an Outrageous Lover. An Outrageous Lover means we get over the hurt, we get over the contraction, we find our way in, and we step up in full resplendent glory because:

- We all know contractions.
- We all know pain.
- We all know hurt.
- We all know the feeling of emptiness.
- We all know the feeling of being alone

It's different for everyone. For some people, the feeling they have is *I am not recognized enough*. Spiritual teachers have that all the time. It is hard for them to listen to other people talk. It is like *wow, I am not recognized; I am not talking.*

Everyone has their version of that, in every profession, in every walk of life.

When we're really in our Unique Self, we can be delighted when we hear someone else.

When we are in our separate self, we have to grasp for space. **When I'm in my Unique Self, I'm in devotion to someone else's Unique Self**. In order for us to be an Outrageous Lover, this means:

> I love you.
> I want to hear you.
> I am devoted to you.
> I adore you.

To truly adore someone, not as an extension of ourselves, but by delving into the details of their life and deeply feeling their pain and joy, we must become an Outrageous Lover, not an ordinary lover.

An ordinary lover uses another person as an extension of who they are because they do not feel their own uniqueness.

But when we're in our enlightened experience, we can feel our uniqueness and invite others' uniqueness—and we are looking here for the democratization of enlightenment. Our first code reaches for the democratization of greatness, the democratization of enlightenment.

Deep in the *dharma*, deep in the code—this is a code of Cosmos—deep in the code of uniqueness is that *only if I am in my uniqueness for real do I have space for you.* **Only if I am in my uniqueness for real, am I connected; my uniqueness is the currency of connection.** Separate self means *separate from.* I am *separate from.*

If I am *separate from,* I can only access the love in myself, which is ordinary love. But if I'm unique, I'm connected to All-That-Is, and the love in my *Self* is Outrageous Love.

It is the same love that is the initiating and animating Eros of All-That-Is that lives in me, as me, and through me.

That's the code. It's when we are in separate self that we cannot find that, and we just have ordinary love. When we're in Unique Self, we understand that uniqueness is the currency of connection, and uniqueness is the puzzle piece that connects us to All-That-Is.

YOUR UNIQUE SELF IS LIKE PLUGGING INTO THE COSMOS

Here's an image to get what Unique Self is like:

- It is like an electrical cord, and at the end of the electrical cord we have a plug, and that plug plugs into the wall, and that plug is our Unique Self.
- Our separate self cannot plug into the wall.
- Our True Self does not plug into the wall.
- Our separate self has two kinds of prongs, but they don't fit.
- At the end of our True Self, we are part of the one—we just have a little round thing, but there are no prongs at all to fit into the wall because it is all one.
- Only if I am a Unique Self do we have a cord, and at the end of the cord, we have this plug that is *precisely unique that plugs into the evolutionary source*, the Outrageous Love source of all Cosmos. Then that love—as Outrageous Love—not as ordinary love, pours into us. We receive it, and we can be devoted.

We do not want to just receive that Outrageous Love to use it and write it someplace. We receive it because we are awake, alive, and delighted. We are Outrageous Lovers. We are delighted by you. To be an Outrageous Lover means I'm delighted by you.

To be unique means we can pray because we affirm the dignity of our personal need, and *my* personal is part of a larger, seamless coat of the universe.

Who are you? I'm a unique expression of the LoveIntelligence and LoveBeauty that is the initiating and animating energy of All-That-Is that lives in me, as me, and through me, that never was, is, or will be ever again, and to know that is my identity.

Oh my God, I'm at home in the universe. I'm connected; I'm a puzzle piece connected to everything. Everything connects through me. I connect through everything. We are so deep in our uniqueness that we have room for other people.

Here's the thing. We can have a person who is a really powerful separate self, and they are doing their mission—but it *is* all about them. It doesn't matter if you are: a plumber, a doctor, a lawyer, or a schoolteacher.

As a separate self, it is only about *you*.

Here's the paradox. If I am really in my Unique Self, I have all the room in the world for you:

- I can listen to you.
- I can hear you.
- I can empathize with you.
- I can taste you.
- I can love you.

That is the test of Unique Self. The great Reality is a trickster.

Love is Outrageous Love—and Outrageous Love is the love of a Unique Self—which can love the other person open. You can completely tell the difference between someone who loves you as an extension of themselves—which is lovely—but someone who is loving you, who feels you, sees you, is committed to you,

A Unique Self can be a lover.

76

A Unique Self can give their gift.

A Unique Self is at home, delighted, awake, and alive.

Let's pray together a prayer we borrowed from the band Foreigner long ago. We revised their song "I Want to Know What Love Is" as a prayer, spoken as a Unique Self fully awake and alive. Amen. Take it away in Bethlehem, and all over the world.

UNIQUE SELVES BAND TOGETHER AS A UNIQUE SELF SYMPHONY

We are the band of Outrageous Lovers. We are the Unique Self Symphony rising from love. This is Bethlehem. And this church has to spread beyond the six thousand gorgeous, awesome, Unique Selves in this Unique Self Symphony. In order to be a force of transformation, there have to be six million people in this church.

For the first time, the world is rising as a self-organizing universe of Unique Selves into a gorgeous Unique Self Symphony.

What does it mean to be a member of an Evolutionary Church of Outrageous Lovers? This is no small membership where you get to be member of this or that. It means we are the first members of an Evolutionary Church that is at this moment of a planetary shift.

The situation has not been resolved as to which way we're going to go: toward a more devolutionary scenario or existential exponential innovation and creativity. **What will make the difference? Membership in a spiritually motivated expression of evolutionary creative life—action out there, working in the world—could well be critical.**

It could be critical, whatever the numbers of people wanting to be part of this by becoming members of a body. The difference between an isolated cell and a cell as a member of an eye is that the single-celled eye could not see. A single-cell thumb could not lift. None of it can work. But by developing a membership, a collective, it means each person becomes a member of a new whole.

That's how things happen. If I am a member of a single cell, I can only do so much. But if I am a member of a multicellular organism, I can fly, I can talk, I can move.

If we are single members of a small church, that is one thing. But if we're members of an Evolutionary Church that's growing to include everybody who would like to be part of it, everyone is always welcome at Evolutionary Church.

To be a member is taking the next step and saying, *We are standing for this; this is ours. We are not just attending. We are going to build this, together, over time.*

CHAPTER FIVE

REALITY NEEDS YOUR SERVICE: THE SEVEN Ss AND KABBALAH IN A SELF-ORGANIZING UNIVERSE

Episode 47 — September 16, 2017

EACH OF US IS ENCODED IN THE PLANETARY BODY

Here is our Evolutionary Love code:

> You are a Unique Self.
>
> You are an irreducibly unique expression of the LoveIntelligence and LoveBeauty that is the initiating and animating energy of All-That-Is.
>
> As such, you have an irreducible unique perspective, a unique quality of intimacy, a unique taste that is unlike any that ever was, is, or has been ever again, and. . .
>
> Your unique taste is needed by All-That-Is.

It is a miracle to imagine that every single person on this Earth is needed uniquely and that we are each one of those. What is the possible field in which this could be true? **Nature's ability is amazing to form whole system bodies like our own with trillions of cells, each unique and each playing a role.**

If you are an eye cell in a little fetus and you are transplanted to the toe in the earliest days of the fetus, you might try to build a toe. But once the little organism has matured and you plant your eye cell into the toe, you continue to try to build an eye.

The same is true of the "imaginal discs" in the body of the caterpillar. When the discs first come into the caterpillar, they do not know who they are. They are all mixed up, and they are often killed by the body of the caterpillar until they discover that every one of them is coded with a unique part of the butterfly that they are to build.

As things get nearer to emerging the butterfly, as each unique part gets close, then if I am to be a whisker, I'll get really excited because I'm innately a whisker.

Here's the thought: Even if every one of us is coded with the part of the planetary body—the social body that we are to play—it's very hard in our early days to imagine that we are playing a unique part in the living organism of a planet that is just awakening to its wholeness.

But as we get closer and closer to the moment of planetary coordination by the higher power—the God power, the amazing self-organizing Godhead of the universe—each person's uniqueness starts to show up. **If you are being transplanted to do something that isn't yours to do, you are going to be miserable.** If you are anywhere near what you are supposed to be doing, it is like you are getting hot on the trail of communion and coordination and giving your gift.

We are getting hot on the trail by being supra-sexually aroused because each of us in this church is nearer and nearer to the planetary birth and to our unique part in it.

I would like to say a prayer that everybody in the church, starting with this small group of human beings, the thousands of us, will dedicate ourselves to knowing that every one of us is unique. Every one of us has a gorgeous, unique role to play.

We are being guided by the God-Force and the great creating process to get closer and closer to that uniqueness in the social body.

How do we feel when we are getting closer?

> Pleasure.
> Joy.
> Attraction.
> Affirmation.

It's the promise of ever closer resonance within the social body.

YOUR UNIQUE TASTE IS NEEDED BY ALL-THAT-IS

We are celebrating the week before Lisa's wedding at Evolutionary Church. And we are celebrating as we are all getting married to each other. But we are getting married in a different way—not as romantic lovers, as Outrageous Lovers, because that is who we are. We are Outrageous Lovers.

To be an Outrageous Lover is to know the LoveIntelligence of Reality. **LoveIntelligence of Reality is not ordinary love; it's the allurement whose feeling is pleasure that awakens uniquely as you.** It awakens uniquely as Barbara.

And here's the strange paradox of Reality which is going to bring us towards our field of prayer. Barbara and Marc are exactly the same—99% of our DNA code, the same. Same organs, not all the same organs but mostly. We are basically the same. Yet, that last percent of DNA structure is utterly and irreducibly unique.

When you think about anyone doing what they're here to do, you get a taste of who they are. Here at Evolutionary Church, you taste Marc-ness. Then you taste Barbara-ness. We call that your unique taste. We are not confused with each other. We do not think *that feels like Barbara*, or *it feels like Marc*. Nothing confusing about it at all. Notice that it is immediately clear.

Try and call up your own unique taste—that is harder because self-love is harder.

> *Being able to call up our own unique taste is the beginning of self-love and is the beginning of enlightenment.*

We call up our own unique taste from a place where we are utterly delighted and ecstatic because of the unique taste of everyone else.

And here's our code for today:

> You are a Unique Self. You are an irreducibly unique expression of the LoveIntelligence and LoveBeauty that is the initiating and animating energy of All-That-Is.

That is code one. Code two:

> As such, you have an irreducible unique perspective, a unique quality of intimacy, a unique taste that is unlike any that ever was, is, or has been ever again.

That is code two. Evolutionary code three is:

> And your unique taste is needed by All-That-Is.

You are needed. Barbara-ness is needed by All-That-Is, and no matter what Marc tries to do—turn upside-down, do three somersaults, six times an hour—I (Marc) will not be able to give to Reality the unique gift that Reality needs that can only be given by Barbara-ness.

And here's the crazy, wild, beautiful thing. It is not just true about Barbara-ness, it's true about each of us.

Is that true? Could it be true that there are these seven billion people, that there is a multiplying miracle of uniqueness in Reality? Could it be that seven billion people irreducibly matter? It is true. It is utterly true, and it is reflected in our molecular structures, our DNA structures, and our cellular structures.

Know what that means? That means that there is nothing extra in our lives.

I (Marc) was thinking of moving to Sunrise Ranch, and Barbara and I spent a lot of time working on this. We spent months on it, investing time and energy.

In the end, it seemed to be the wrong thing to do, and we decided to set up other offices. But all the time we spent working on Sunrise Ranch was not a mistake. It was not an accident. It was beautiful, and it was necessary. Then I realized, oh my God, every place I have been, I need to be—every detour is a destination, and whatever the crisis is, that crisis births something new.

Every crisis is an evolutionary driver. What a beautiful thing to say. Every crisis opens us up to transformation.

In Hebrew, the word for crisis is *sheber*. *Sheber* means the nourishment needed to survive, and it means crisis, both.

I love to quote Barbara, and she loves to quote me because we are joining genius, and we can get to a place of being egoless, where I say *Reality needs Barbara*. I can be in devotion to Barbara-ness, and we can be whole mates; we can vision the world together, and we can join genius.

How exciting is this? It means that our holy and our broken *Hallelujah* is all part of the story. Nothing is left out. Have I experienced a holy and a broken *Hallelujah*? Of course I have. Has Barbara? Of course she has.

We know that there is nothing more whole than a broken heart, and there is nothing more holy than a broken heart. **Every yearning, every deep and true yearning, is holy.** It is evolution's yearning, and we get to be in this place where we bring everything, and we lay it on her altar, on the altar of She. Everything. Nothing's left out.

From that place of fullness, from that place of *Hallelujah*—which means drunken intoxication and pristine praise—we bring it all to God, not the god who is Santa Claus, but God who is the Infinity of Intimacy that knows our name.

Evolutionary Church is about the evolution of God. We need to reclaim God. And Evolutionary Church is about the evolution of prayer. We need to reclaim prayer. **Prayer affirms the dignity of our personal stories and the dignity of personal need. From that place, as my master the Baal Shem Tov said,** *we ask for everything.*

We enter our hymn as we do every week, as we evolve the source code together and gather thousands of us from all over the world. We step into the holy and the broken, *Hallelujah*.

We bring all of our tears and all of our delight and all of our ecstasy and all of our joy. *Do not be a spectator to all time and existence*, as the Greeks said. Let's pray and ask for everything.

I want to invite everybody, do not skip the prayer.

I know that there are some of us who kind of stay on the side and read other people's prayers, which is beautiful. But when I actually speak my prayer and impress my prayer on the lips of the Divine, when I offer up my holy and broken *Hallelujah*, and when I confess my prayer and vulnerability, it is not the same as thinking it.

Speech, the act of speaking, is received by the Infinity of Intimacy in a new and gorgeous way.

We seed the Earth with a new vision together, all of us, as they did in Bethlehem, *amen. Amen.*

THE SEVEN Ss OF UNIQUENESS: HOW THE UNIVERSE SELF-ORGANIZES

The social technologies which the creative process of the universe uses to help us become unique within the whole are called the Seven Ss.

SYNTENY

Synteny is an attunement with the patterns of creation experienced as one's own inner motivation and intuition. With synteny, we are attuning. It's almost like there is a DNA in there that the RNA uses to build a body. If you have ever attuned to that deep inner impulse through prayer, through meditation, through asking, it will be there because it is coming from a deeper part than your mental mind or even your spiritual intuition. Attunement comes through synteny.

SYNERGY

Synergy is the coming together of separate parts to form a new whole different from, greater than, and unpredictable from the sum of the parts. Two or more cells come together, and multicellular organisms begin to form. **As organisms form, they get newer and newer as they get more and more complex with each cell taking up its own unique impulse.** This is so gorgeous. This is like how God works.

SYNCHRONICITY

Synchronicity, the third S, is the apparent acausal relationship. How is it that we happen to have met each other? How did I (Barbara) happen to meet Marc, who came and said, *Let's do an interview*. I sat down with him, never thought about him, started to talk, this happened, that happened. Carl Jung thought it was the fourth power of the universe that it should have designed these specifics. Here's the way Carl Jung writes it: *the apparent acausal relationship among events*. It's coincidences that could not be planned by the human mind, but that appear to flow from a larger and more comprehensive design.

Let's say that when we have a chance meeting and are now looking to join genius, we are looking for where we fit best.

Be very sensitive to shared contacts with surprising people and always look upon them as *vitally interesting and a surprise*.

It's not that everyone will be your partner. Out of synchronicity, as we climb the mountain of evolution from a base where we hardly meet anybody, if we keep climbing, we get closer and closer to the top of that mountain, and we get to meet almost everybody that we need to meet.

In the Evolutionary Church, we are climbing to the top of the mountain because people are already self-selected to be here. Anybody we meet in this church is part of an organic connection to you, through you, through their own synergy and synteny.

SUPRA-SEX

Supra-sex, the fourth S, is the passion to express unique creativity stimulated by vocational arousal. I am so vocationally aroused thinking of supra-sex, the passion to express my unique creativity stimulated by being with all of you who might like to have it.

I (Barbara) was in fact in the wrong place, when I tried to do this in the Church Women United or the General Federation of Women's Clubs when I was younger. I wanted to give my unique gift over there. Do you think it was able to be given? No, it was the wrong group. Supra-sex is the passion to express unique creativity stimulated by vocational arousal in this church, comparable to sexual.

---

*Instead of joining genes to procreate,
we are joining genius to co-create.*

Nature has had to put some excitement into joining genius so that we will not only be joining genes to have more babies, but we'll be joining genius to give birth to our greater selves. Nature's passion here is to make joining genius and vocational arousal so supra-sexy that people will do almost anything to be able to get that done.

SYNTROPY

Syntropy, the fifth S, is nature's tendency to form whole systems of increasing complexity, consciousness, and freedom. While entropy represents disorder, nature has spent billions of years creating higher order through syntropy. She does this by connecting individuals attracted to each other to create.

Nature develops syntropy through supra-sexual joining, out of the synchronicity of getting closer to each other, by the design of evolution, feeling that the separate parts are forming something great. Your syntony, the harmonic inside you, is being resonant with your action.

SPONTANEITY

Spontaneity is next. This is really great. This gathering is not totally planned. In fact, almost none of it is planned. Yet we have the codes we know we are going to do; we are not sure exactly who is here, but let's assume that it is exactly right.

Spontaneity is the experience of unpremeditated action and thought that flows naturally without thinking or planning. As we get closer and closer to being like this, we think less, and we express more spontaneously.

SELF-CREATIVITY

The seventh S is self-creativity: who is doing all this? The tendency in nature to organize itself is called "autopoiesis,"[11] the inherent capacity in nature to self-organize without apparent outside manipulation. We do not have a god that is forcing it; it springs from the Field of Universal Intelligence out of which everything is arising.

---

11 *Autopoiesis* is a concept originating from biology and philosophy, introduced by Chilean biologists Humberto Maturana and Francisco Varela in the 1970s. The term is derived from the Greek words *auto* (self) and *poiesis* (creation or production), meaning self-creation or self-producing. It describes the ability of a system to maintain and reproduce itself through its internal processes and interactions with its environment.

Let's breathe into that and realize an awesome appreciation of the invisible process of creation, the evolutionary godhead, creating out in a totally hidden manner through all of the particles until we arise up to the universal humans like ourselves, the evolutionary humans.

We are beginning to make the invisible God visible internally and externally through love.

Some people live with the seven Ss printed on their wall. It would be interesting as we teach here to refer every now and then to one of the Ss, because they deepen us in being the exact imprint of God.

We are going to fit this together.

We are going to join genius right now, in this very second, spontaneously and synergistically creating a new synteny which allows us to do something that has never been done before. We are going to do public supra-sex, synchronously.

Let's summarize this into one sentence each.

- Synteny—attunement with the patterns of creation experienced as one's inner motivation and intuition.
- Synergy—the coming together of separate parts to form a new whole, different and greater than the sum of the parts.
- Synchronicity—the apparent acausal relationship among events. Acausal means that it looks like it is not connected, but it actually is. It is all happening with great intention.
- Supra-sex—the passion to express unique creativity stimulated by vocational arousal.
- Syntropy—nature's tendency to form whole systems of greater complexity, consciousness, and freedom. Entropy is a devolved syntropy.
- Spontaneity—the experience of unpremeditated actions and thoughts flowing naturally without thinking.
- Self-creativity—the tendency to organize itself through

autopoiesis, the inherent capacity in nature to self-organize without apparent outside manipulation.

GOD NEEDS YOUR SERVICE: KABBALAH AND THE SEVEN Ss

Now let's bring the seven Ss in complete, synchronous synergy with (and we are going to do this spontaneously) an act of supra-sex, a new alignment with the deeper synteny of Reality as Reality self-organizes through our self-creativity.

Let's make this happen right now, and let's do it by merging these seven Ss through our Evolutionary Love code of this week which is:

> You are needed by All-That-Is. Your irreducibly unique intelligence, your irreducibly unique LoveIntelligence and LoveBeauty, is needed by All-That-Is.

Let's really feel this and feel how this expresses itself through our evolutionary code.

I am going to give it to you in the sixteenth century proto-evolutionary thinking of the *Kabbalah.*

Kabbalah is the only great mystical system that's evolutionary. That's really important to understand. In Germany, Fichte and Schelling,[12] in pages of scholarly footnotes on this in the books of Eliot Wolfson,[13] are drawing on Luria's *Kabbalah.*

Luria's *Kabbalah,* at its core, is evolutionary. It's different than Buddhism, different even than *Kashmir Shaivism.* It understands Reality as being a

---

12   Johann Gottlieb Fichte and Friedrich Wilhelm Joseph Schelling were German philosophers associated with German Idealism, a philosophical movement that arose in the late 18th and early 19th centuries following the work of Immanuel Kant.

13   Elliot R. Wolfson (born November 23, 1956) is a distinguished scholar specializing in Jewish mysticism, philosophy, and comparative mysticism. He holds the Marsha and Jay Glazer Endowed Chair in Jewish Studies and serves as a Distinguished Professor of Religion at the University of California, Santa Barbara.

pulse that is evolving, moving forward. Luria had a very deep understanding of cultural evolution but didn't yet have the science of evolution in the biosphere.

Obviously, he did not know about the Big Bang, but he understood that Reality is not eternity, that Reality is evolving and that we are personally implicated—evolution lives in us. That is core to Luria's thought, and to Fichte and Schelling.

The founders of evolutionary spirituality are drawing from *Kabbalah*, which is completely fascinating. *Kabbalah* is a proto-evolutionary system, just like there are *prokaryotes* from Latin; *pro* means before; and *karyote* means the kernel. Prokaryote is a cell before it has a nucleus. Proto-evolution means the evolutionary idea before it is formally in the world, already lives in *Kabbalah*.

In *Kabbalah*, in the sixteenth century, an Italian man named Ibn Gabbai[14] says, *avodah tzarech Kabbalah*—"God needs your service."

And by God, he doesn't mean Santa Claus. He means the incessant creativity of Cosmos in its personal face that knows your name, that holds you personally. The Infinity of Intimacy needs your partnership, needs your quality of intimacy.

Let's bring this together with the seven Ss. It's very beautiful to really understand it.

What does synteny mean?

Synteny means that in Reality:

- There is a system in which everything is related.
- There is a harmony.
- There is orchestration happening in the deepest structure of Reality.

---

14   Meir ben Ezekiel ibn Gabbai was a prominent 16th-century Kabbalist born in Spain around 1480.

- There is an inner orchestra.
- There is an inner symphony that is happening all the time.

One of the properties of synteny is synergy.

Synergy means that these separate parts, you and me, are unique separate parts. We are unique because only by Barbara and Marc joining uniquely and then joining uniquely with others, can we create a new whole.

One example of that new whole is Evolutionary Church. Evolutionary Church is an expression of the synteny of Reality that is moving towards new synergies, which are wholes greater than the sum of the parts.

It manifests through synchronicity, which brings the irreducible uniqueness of Barbara, together with the irreducible uniqueness of Marc, together with the irreducible uniqueness of others.

There is no church without each one of us.

Synchronicity brings us all together. Just think about synchronicity for a second and all the holy and broken *Hallelujahs* it took to bring us here to this place—all of the crises that it took to create the transformations needed. It is the new synergy that emerges from this whole, and then supra-sex happens—joining genius happens.

Supra-sex is the allurement that takes place between what we call whole mates. **Whole mates are people who are not just looking deeply in each other's eyes; they are also looking at a shared horizon; they are committed to the whole.**

Barbara and I are committed together to the whole, and we are committed to being aligned with the synteny of Reality to produce a new synergy, honoring the synchronicity of us coming together, and then supra-sex, joining genius, to create something new, potent, and powerful that was not here before. When that happens, we allow our spontaneity to happen, which is the code for this week: *you are needed by All-That-Is.*

We are going to spontaneously merge this evolutionary code with the seven Ss in this exact moment, and that creates the sense of self-creativity.

Self-creativity emerges and manifests in this self-organizing Reality and creates syntropy, which is Reality evolving to higher wholes.

Oh my God, it just happened—right here, right now. That was beautiful. I never thought we could do it that fast.

It can only happen if we are loving each other. Only Outrageous Love allows us to be talking. It is only from a place of this kind of egoless Outrageous Love that we are able to make this happen. Here we are creating it together in this moment. Right here. Right now.

But we cannot bypass the personal:

> Barbara is here because her dad was a toy king, and she had this complex relationship with him that she had to try and work out. Some of her siblings worked it out, and some of them did not. It was the male side of things. It was only working through everything that created her commitment to Conscious Evolution.

> Marc also has to bring his entire holy and broken *Hallelujah* to the story. His mother is a Holocaust survivor. She's in Poland right now. His father, bless him, is who his father is with all of the complexity. Nothing's left out.

What it means is we do not live in our wounding. We do not view our wounding as this tragedy that gives us our identity.

Our wounding is the ground of our emergence.

---

*Our wounding is part of the symphony
of Cosmos, it is part of the synchronicity,
and it creates the new synergy.*

We bring our holy and our broken *Hallelujah*, because if we do not do that, we become pathological. Communism has had bad forms of evolutionary spirituality, and yes, there are bad forms of evolutionary spirituality, like there are shadow forms of church, and there are shadow forms of New Age.

If we do not work out our personal stuff, we bypass it, and then what happens is that the pathology explodes, and instead of evolutionary spirituality healing Reality, it creates communism, which devastated Reality. And instead of the church creating kindness and ethics, we have New Age systems that create shadow and attack.

We have to live a sacred universe together, and we only do that by walking through our emptiness, by being able to tell everyone what I (Marc) love most about Barbara Marx Hubbard. I shouldn't share something so private in public, but I am going to.

There are about thirty things, but honestly what I love most is that Barbara is always transforming. Barbara never says, *I am done.*

You would think that when she had just hit age 89, she would say, *I am done. I am done, I am 89, I am done*—but she never does. She is always amazing, and I hope that is what Barbara and I share.

Six weeks ago, when I was on a plane, Barbara said, *Marc, Could you do this thing in our conversations?*

I said, *Thank you so much, that is such good feedback. I did not realize that.*

I didn't say, *No, it is not that way.* I said, *Thank you.* I love Barbara even more for pointing out to me that I could be better this way.

It is that fearless egolessness that is the ground of Outrageous Love.

As teachers, we do not have to model perfection.

- We can model making mistakes in the right direction.
- We can be strong by being vulnerable.
- We can be holy by bringing our holy and our broken *Hallelujah.*

I had planned to talk about *Reality needs your service*, but after hearing Barbara's seven Ss, I can say, *I am going to talk about that instead. That is so good. Let's merge with seven Ss.*

That is Outrageous Love, my friends.

CHAPTER SIX

WE PARTNER WITH GOD AND FIND OUR PLACE AS A CO-CREATOR

Episode 48 — September 23, 2017

ALL-THAT-IS NEEDS YOUR UNIQUENESS

Evolutionary Love Code:

> You are needed by All-That-Is.

This is the most beautiful thought! I really love this thought, being needed by All-That-Is. I would like to invite you to put your attention on what it is you most need to give. Feel its essence, the uniqueness of what you *most* need to give, and then place your attention on *where it is most needed,* and imagine it being received in the fullness of your ability to give it. That process activates the life energy of each of us to the fullest degree and towards giving it to the world. As we give it to the world, we are receiving it. **This deep reality—giving our needed gift where it is received—is both our greatest gift to others and to ourselves. It is self-rewarding.**

This phrase, *you are uniquely needed,* is very important here. That's what it means to step into our code and to step into Evolutionary Church. Remember our previous code:

> You are an irreducible Unique Self. You are an irreducible, unique expression of the

LoveIntelligence and LoveBeauty of All-That-Is. That means you have a unique quality of intimacy, and you have a unique quality of presence that never was, is, or will be ever again, other than through you.

Each one of these codes is critical.

You have a unique quality of intimacy and unique quality of presence. Those two come together—and they create your unique capacity—your unique gift to address a unique need in the world that no one else can meet.

Again, you are an irreducible, unique expression of the LoveIntelligence and LoveBeauty of All-That-Is. This means:

- I'm not just a separate self—I am not just a skin-encapsulated ego.
- I'm part of the Field of LoveIntelligence and LoveBeauty— I'm part of the Field of Consciousness.
- I'm not separate from the field.
- I'm a unique expression of the field.

That is the first code. The second code is—I mean, it's very beautiful, we just see the codes emerging—you have a unique quality of presence, you have a quality of intimacy that is unlike anyone's that ever was, is, or will be. You have a unique perspective.

Wow. You have a unique *perspective*!

Those three things, **you have a unique quality of presence, a unique quality of intimacy, a unique perspective.** That is code two.

Code three:

As such, you have a unique gift that no one that ever was, is, or will be, has.

We just asked ourselves gorgeously in the resonant field to feel into *what I want to give*. Then we said something else, which was the fourth code, and the fourth code is:

> It is not just that you have a unique gift. You can *express your gift*. It is not just about self-expression. It is not just about Reality manifesting, not just about manifesting even *as* you. It is your gift.

YOUR UNIQUE GIFT IS NEEDED BY ALL-THAT-IS

Code four is *you are needed by All-That-Is*. Oh my God. **All-That-Is needs your service.** I mean, to really get that! That's the experience we call in Evolutionary Church, the "Barack Obama Experience," and with all great respect for President Trump, we have kept it as the Barack Obama Experience.

> Barack Obama calls you and says, *Oh my god, you're Barbara Marx Hubbard. Oh my God, I totally need you. I can't move anything forward without you.*
>
> And Barbara says, *Do you even know me? I mean, you probably just know my brother-in-law, Daniel Ellsberg because he was doing the Pentagon papers.*
>
> Obama answers, *No, no, no, no, Barbara. Forget Daniel. I know he has a new book out on nuclear issues, which is a great book. I just read it, but actually Barbara, you are the one I need!*

Then he knows everything about Barbara: her dad was a toy maker, about her relationship with Sidney; I mean, he knows everything! That means he really knows her, and he says, *Barbara, you are the only one who can help me.*

And Barbara gets off the phone. Is she depressed? Is Barbara depressed? No! Barbara is *ecstatic* because Barack Obama just called and said, *I need you.*

The feeling of being needed is an ecstatic feeling, and Barack Obama is *calling* each one of us, and saying, *I need you. I need you in church. I can't do church without you.* We need each other.

Or let's take the celebration of a wedding. Imagine someone's wedding day. What is the celebration of a wedding? It is the realization that bride and groom say to each other, *I need you. I need you.* That is an incredible thing to say.

We have turned need into codependency, and we believe that if you need someone, you are codependent, and there is something wrong with you.

All your friends come to rescue you. Oh my God. *I need someone.* Really? Well, we can turn to each other here and say *I need you.*

I can't do it without you.

I am not codependent.

I don't need to be rescued.

We are delighted to need each other. I'm ecstatic!

To need each other is to find our divinity because the deepest mystical truth is that Infinite Divinity, the Infinity of Intimacy, God, who we call in church the Infinity of Intimacy, needs you. We have two names for God in church: the Possibility of Possibility and the Infinity of Intimacy. As we are trying to re-language Reality, those are our two names for God. The Infinity of Intimacy and the Possibility of Possibility turns to each of us and says, *I need you!* Like at a wedding, when people can break open enough, and bride and groom can turn to each other and say, *I need you.*

Let's have a wedding right now. Let's turn to each other and say: *I need you.* We turn to one another and say: *We need you. I need you.* **When we are able to say, *I need you*, we are able to break open into our vulnerability.** When I say, *I need you*, I bring with me my holy and my broken *Hallelujah*, I bring *the whole story* with me. Nothing is left out. All of me needs all of you, and all of Reality needs each of us. My friends, when a couple is getting married, we are going to get married with them. We are going to say to God, *God, I need you.* And God's saying to each of us, *I need you. I need you.*

---

*God is saying to you, I need you!
That is the experience of being
God's Evolutionary Lover.*

We are joining genius with the Divine as we join genius with each other, and we can only do it if we break open, not only in our greatness, but in our vulnerability.

We bring our *Hallelujahs* before the Divine, our holy and our broken *Hallelujah*. We pray for everything while we listen to Leonard Cohen's "Hallelujah."

> *Hallelujah! And even though it all went wrong I'll stand before
> the Lord of Song with nothing on my tongue but Hallelujah.*

We are not praying to the Santa Claus god; we are not praying to the puppeteer god. We are praying to the **God who is the Infinity of Intimacy that both lives in us and holds us**. When Rumi says, *Let me fall into the arms of the Beloved*, Rumi is talking about the Infinity of Intimacy that knows our name, and prayer affirms the dignity of personal need. Prayer affirms the dignity of personal need. When we pray, we just ask God: *God, we need you!* We ask for *everything. When you pray,* the holy Baal Shem Tov, *Ask for everything!* We pray for all of humanity and for our individual needs, and we pray for worldwide intentions. But don't skip yourself! We don't bypass ourselves, my friends, we pray for everything; we pray for everyone.

When I grow in my consciousness, I find my truest need, and I don't bypass my personal need. Prayer affirms the dignity of my need.

I need to know that I am needed by All-That-Is, that the world cannot live without me. Without me, there is no world; there is no Eros. It is not alive without me or without you; it is not happening without you and me. Our first message here was: *God is lonely.* **It is only when I get that God needs my service, that the Infinity of Intimacy needs me, that the dignity of my own need is affirmed.** When I know I am needed, then my own need becomes dignified, and I can storm the heavens and demand that my need is addressed with such dignity, with such grace. *Amen.*

FINDING THE PLACE WHERE I FIT BEST IS KEY FOR THE NEW HUMAN

We are a church of new humans. There is a special requirement for new humans to know how needed they are to give their gift. First of all, what is a new human? I believe it is somebody who is picking up the impulse of evolution within themselves. We're picking up the impulse of evolution within ourselves such that this impulse is awakening us, activating us to become something more, something new, something that maybe doesn't totally fit in the existing world as it is. In other words, new humans are builders of a new world.

New humans are motivated by the ever evolving impulse of creation to be more.

If I am motivated to be more than what was existing before—certainly in me or others near me—I have to find, first of all, what it is I am yearning to give, and secondly, where it fits best. I (Barbara) have mentioned in other sermons that Jonas Salk told me it is not *survival of the fittest but survival of what fits best.* **If you have a deep inner impulse, a need to give and it doesn't feel to you that it is fitting anywhere yet, it's very hard to give it the whole way.** You have to be extremely courageous to do that, and you have to keep seeking as to where it fits.

I will tell you a brief personal story, because I was so stuck. For the first years of my adult marriage, from 1951 to about 1958, I did not know where I fit, and if you can imagine I was trying to! I had an evolutionary impulse, but I didn't know its name. I was trying to give that evolutionary impulse in the Church Women United or the General Federation of Women's Clubs or the local school board, and you know what? It didn't fit. I didn't feel needed by All-That-Is. I didn't *know* that I was needed by All-That-Is.

As a new human, what we have to do, in order for this to be emotionally true, is we have to realize that we are All-That-Is *becoming*. We are not all-that-structurally-exists. If I wanted to be myself, I couldn't join an ordinary church, I couldn't go and study to be a doctor or a lawyer in the old structure. **We are a church of new humans who are motivated deeply within to give their gift into an emerging world.**

This brings me to the word vocation. It is one thing to say we are needed by All-That-Is, but you are needed for a *uniqueness*. Everyone is a unique expression of the process of creation. We must know that uniqueness, feel it and, find where it fits best is the work of the new humans. This is in many respects the work of the new church, of the Evolutionary Church, because we are gathered here together to give our gift to the evolution of ourselves and our world. Part of our work is to find out where we all fit. Is that true? Do you know where you fit best?

You fit best where people are yearning for the gift that you uniquely are.

When I first met my whole mate, I had never met anyone who really needed my gift fully. Fully! Nor had I met anyone whose gift I fully needed, in a way that was resonant with what I wanted to give. You see, nature must have worked this out in physical bodies because we get fertilized as a little egg and then gradually the eye-cell knows to build an eye, the ear-cell knows to build an ear.

Realize the exquisite refinement of the bodies, that every single cell is unique and knows where it fits. I am asking a question of the Evolutionary Church: *How do we know where we fit best?* For me, it was one thing to

101

know what I wanted to give, but it was very hard for me to know where I fit best. The process of knowing where you fit best in order to give your gift takes a couple of things:

Knowing where I fit best takes a deep internal faith *that I am needed,* **even though it may not look that way.** If I am not being affirmed by the outside world, I have to have some faith inside me. This we can give each other in the church, even if the gift is not fully recognizable yet. Sometimes one must create the space where one's unique gift fits best—this is very true. You have to create the space where you are needed and where your gift is needed and is therefore encouraged.

That is a great function of the Evolutionary Church, to help each of us know where we fit best and then to give it. We realize that when we are giving our gift as a new human where it fits best, it isn't fitting into the old structures. It's not fitting in the sense of being a leader of the power system as it now exists. In order for us to find where we fit best and to give our gift, we have to be pioneers to some degree because we are creating the spaces where we fit. The spaces where you fit are the new structures of society in which you fit best. This is a big story.

What do you experience when you fit best? How do you know that you have found where you fit best? How do you know how to give thanks for fitting best?

The giving of your unique vocation is joy. I call it the compass of joy.

If you need to have some guide as to where you fit best, you can scan for your inner impulse of joy, wherever you are feeling it and with whom you are feeling it.

You are being guided by that love to go more toward giving your gifts where you are loved and loving and where you need and are needed. This means in order to give your gift where it is most needed, you have to find where you are most loved and most needed yourself, and sometimes that takes years and years and years.

When I (Barbara) went to Bryn Mawr College—I will never forget that—I was sitting there, and I was looking at this huge curriculum survey as to what do I want to major in. I had no idea. I remember saying, *I think I'll go get a job in Washington.* That is about how deep it was.

So, I majored in political science. That was stupid! I mean, not that it wasn't a nice thing to do, but I didn't know! I went back to Bryn Mawr 50 years after having graduated, and I said to the girls, *I wonder if now you help students find out what they really need to give, what their vocation is.* They said, *No, there is no interest in it!* In order to realize we are being needed by All-That-Is, we have to tune into that vocation.

We have to realize we are needed by All-That-Is *becoming.*

We are needed by what isn't quite yet there. We have to have the courage to affirm it, and we need to belong to a collective of people who support us to do that so that we are not alone in the search.

How many millions and millions of people are alone in the search as to where to give their gift! One of the great functions of the Evolutionary Church is attracting new humans who want to give a greater gift than society has asked them for. We ask for it. We in the Evolutionary Church ask each other to give that gift, and we want to recognize each other's gifts. We want to feel what we are like when we are giving our gifts, and we want to glorify the gifts of everybody in this church.

HAPPINESS AND JOY ARE A BYPRODUCT OF GIVING MY UNIQUE GIFT

Let's feel into that beautiful word, and let's feel into the different energies of Evolutionary Church. **We want the energy of deep mind, deep intellect,**

new structures, new codes—and we want the energy of ecstasy! We don't want to be afraid of the energy of rapture, of ecstasy, because they are all parts of life. They are all parts of Eros. Often the world of the fundamentalists wants to bypass deep codes, evolution, structures, and enter ecstasy, but then the world of the west-coast liberals are afraid of genuine rapture.

We want to bring them together. We are not afraid of rapture. There is no rupture with rapture in Evolutionary Church. At the same time, we are evolution, and evolution is ecstatic! **Evolution, the feeling of becoming, is not only the feeling of spacious being; it is the feeling of ecstatic urgency.** When we see a kind of *Hallelujah* in the space of fundamentalism, we say, *ah, beware!* But no, no: we want to find the *Hallelujah* and the vibration of a deep truth that arises from our minds and our hearts together.

Let's feel into that space, beloveds. *Life, Liberty, and the pursuit of Happiness.* So good! Life is good; liberty is so beautifully good, but we all know that we can't pursue happiness. When we pursue happiness, we know that happiness always runs in the other direction. What we understand is that happiness and joy is always the byproduct of the passionate pursuit of something else.

Happiness is a byproduct of the passionate pursuit of *something other* **than happiness.** What is it exactly that we were talking about? *Giving my gift, fitting into Reality.* It is not the survival of the fittest, but the survival of that which fits and of that which is needed by All-That-Is.

There is no greater joy than to know that **I am the right person in the right place at the right time**, and joy is the byproduct of the passionate pursuit of giving my gift. Yes! That is the *dharma* of this code. The quality, the experience of living this code that we are talking about is the experience that I am living my gift! I am giving my gift.

When I am giving my gift, it is not that there isn't pain sometimes. It is not that there isn't sometimes even occasionally agony, but:

- I know that I am in my story.

104

- ◆ I know that I am giving my gift.
- ◆ I know that I fit.
- ◆ I know that I belong.

When I know that I belong, when I know that I am in the right story, when I am living the right *why*, then I can bear with almost any *what* that comes up. **When I'm in the wrong story, nothing works.** You get that? When I am in the wrong story just a little pinprick of pain sends me to the roof; I can't handle it, but when I am in the right story, when I am in *my* story—when I know that I am needed by All-That-Is—then everything changes.

I want to introduce a key gorgeous, new way of saying this in Evolutionary Church which is resonant from the field that we are establishing together. You see, there are different models of how we relate to Infinity:

- ◆ We can **ignore Infinity**. We say there is only a material world. That is one model. Bad idea.
- ◆ We can get that **Infinity is our king** and we relate to God as a king or a queen, which people did for many thousands of years, and there is some beauty in that, there is some truth in that.
- ◆ We can say that **Infinity *only lives in* us** and is not *beyond* us. Again, bad idea. We are *not* the whole story. There is the Infinity of Intimacy beyond us.
- ◆ We can look at God or **Infinity as a parent**. There's a parent who loves us and takes care of us.
- ◆ We can look at God or **Infinity as an owner**. We are owned by God, and there is a lot of beauty in all of that, but it is all limited! It is all not quite there. We can't quite feel it.

Let's introduce a new model. This is the partnership model. **We are partners with God.** Wow! Does everyone get the dignity in that? We are God's partner. God needs my service, God needs your service. God needs all of us.

To know that I am God's partner, that God needs my service, that *I can't do it without you*, changes the whole world.

Who is prepared to say *I am God's partner*? Are we willing to change the core model of how I speak to God? **God is not only my king, not only my owner, and not only my parent—but I am God's partner.**

I invite everyone just to step in, in this moment, and write *I am God's partner* and add to it: *God needs me* or *Reality needs me*, whatever works best for you, but find it and speak it out.

I am God's partner. Reality needs me.
I am God's partner. God needs me.

Does everyone get that? *I am God's partner. God needs me.* That changes everything. *I am God's partner, and God needs me. I am God's partner, Reality needs me*, and to *know* that truth. To *know* that truth!

All of a sudden, **I realize *that's why I want to survive*!**

I don't want to survive just because I am a narcissist.

I don't want to survive just because I am selfish.

I want to survive because I'm God's partner, and God needs me! Now, you are going to say, *Is he going to get all excited about that?* Yes, he is! I am! It just blows my heart open. It blows your heart open to realize, oh my God, I am God's partner and Reality *really* needs me! It is true!

CHARITY SAVES FROM DEATH

I'm going to tell you a short story. It is such a great story, and it is so beautiful. I (Marc) received it from my lineage. Oh my God, it's just the most wild story in the world. Here it is:

It is a story that happened on the lower east side of Manhattan.

There was a couple that had come over from Eastern Europe as the Jews came over to America after the pogroms. They were living in a little tenement on the Lower East Side, and they barely had any money. They could barely make it.

They were barely alive. They could barely move, and there were no doctors; there was a lot of sickness and people were dying all around them because of lack of medical care.

In this family there were two daughters who were eleven and ten, and there was a father and mother.

The mother got sick. There were no real hospitals, so the father took the mother to the *hospital*, but it wasn't a hospital. It was like a little room next door with a doctor, who was barely a doctor.

The mother got sicker and sicker, and it came to Friday night which is the Sabbath and the traditional Jewish ritual.

On that Friday night, the father was with the mother, and she passed away. He came home to his little, tiny room with his two daughters who had been waiting all night. They were asleep, and he sat, crying in the corner.

His daughter got up—her name is Sarah—she's eleven or twelve years old. She went and sat on her daddy's lap, and said, *Daddy it's okay. It's okay. Mama is going to be okay.*

The father looked at his daughter and he said, *What do you mean, Mama is going to be okay? What are you saying?*

She replied, *Daddy, we always go to synagogue on Friday night, and you always bring home a guest, and I always ask you why do you bring home a guest, we barely have food for ourselves? And Daddy, Tata, you always say to me, I bring home a guest because charity saves from death.*

Tzedakah tatzil mi'mavet: charity saves from death.

So, Daddy, you know what I did? When you were at the hospital with mama, I went to synagogue, and I brought home a guest, and my little sister and I, we fed the guest because I remembered what you said: Charity saves from death. So, we just gave charity, and charity is going to save Mama from death.

The father looked at his daughter. And friends, open your hearts. The father looked at his daughter, Sarah, and he said:

Sarahle, Sarahle, when I said tzedakah tatzil mi'mavet—charity saves from death—I didn't mean that charity would always save Mama from death.

I meant charity would save God from death.

Charity would save God from death. Wow!

God needs us.

We are God's arms, we are God's verbs, we are God's partners.

When God stands at the abyss of darkness and says, *Let there be light,* God stands at the abyss of a *particular* darkness that *you* stand at, and *I* stand at, and *each one of us* stands at, and *only* at that particular perspective, with the unique quality of intimacy that is *you*, with the unique perspective that is *you*, with the unique gift that is *you*, can God say at *that* place, at *that* abyss of darkness, *Let there be light!*

That is why we understand that *there are unique configurations of light.* And we say in the sacred lineage *ner Elohim nishmat Adam*, the candle of God is the human being, the soul of the human being.

We are the unique frequency of divine light.

God needs our service. **It is our activism that saves God from death, and that is what the Evolutionary Church stands for.** God is our partner, and we are God's partner; we need each other, and we are delighted.

We are so wildly honored to need each other.

THE PURPOSE OF GOD IS TO CREATE CO-CREATORS

I (Barbara) mentioned before, one time I was thanking God, and I talked to God a lot, and I said, *Thank you, God, thank you, thank you, thank you,* and all the things I was thankful for, and God said, *Thank you, Barbara,* which was something of a shock, but then I realized, of course, if I were a parent, and my child was doing well, I would be thanking the child because that is my whole purpose with the child. **A purpose of God that seems to be surfacing in this church is to create co-creators with God.** It's a new relationship to the Divine.

The gift in everybody is the gift given by God. When it is given, it evolves the Godhead, which is now at a time of having to create beings capable of doing this, or else we are going to destroy the Earth.

If we continue to use our power without being partners with the God of a universal evolution, we will misuse the power. I'll just say a little thing about someone I know well, who is writing this book as a nuclear warrior, who says that it is all about thermonuclear war and building more bombs. It is hard to remember, when we are in this church, that they are building more nuclear weapons, and it is hard to realize why and what is happening there while we are doing this over here. It is almost unbelievable that this is *so* in this world.

In this church, we stand with the mission of connecting and collecting new humans worldwide, and if you can, for the moment, allow our mission to fulfill itself in seeing our Evolutionary Church fulfilling itself in our world right now. We are seeing it as a worldwide church. We are seeing many small churches, mosques, temples, cathedrals, but everywhere the new humans are in those churches, partnering with God for the re-creation of a world equal to our potential.

I am speaking for God. He is saying, *Thank you, folks. Thank you, Evolutionary Church.* Let us give our gift to this church, knowing that we are partners with God, feeling thankful that by giving our gift, we're going to realize our whole potential as co-creators with the Divine. **The new human is a co-creator with the Divine.**

Let's feel the ecstasy of knowing that I am taking the whole world in my hands, and we are building it together! Friends, imagine a world in which there are ten million people in Evolutionary Church. Imagine that!

Imagine the vision when all over the world there are Evolutionary Churches meeting virtually, linked to each other, and it is a force of love, of Evolutionary Love in the self-organizing universe that bypasses the deep state, the deep state that is building nuclear bombs. Imagine a force of love, of Evolutionary Love that bypasses the old politics.

Trump, my friends, showed us one thing. He showed us you can bypass the deep state. Trump won the election against sixteen Republican candidates, and then managed to *trump*, as it were, the entire Clinton-Obama machine. That tells us something very powerful. It is the power of self-organization. We might not identify (I certainly don't identify with what Trump is and stands for in any way, sense, shape, or form), but that is not the issue. What he showed us was that something new is possible.

Evolutionary Church needs to become the next vehicle for a politics of Evolutionary Love, for a politics of new candidates, who bypass new candidates at the state, local, representative, and senatorial levels, but not just in America, in every country! **Evolutionary Church should become a political vehicle for a politics of Evolutionary Love.** *Amen!*

And friends, don't be afraid to be ecstatic.

Don't be afraid to be rapturous. No rupture in rapture.

Hallelujah, everyone.

We are needed by All-That-Is!

CHAPTER SEVEN

I AM EVOLUTION, I AM THE GLORY: ACTIVATING OUR GIFTS AT THE FIFTH BIG BANG

Episode 49 — September 30, 2017

YOU ARE BORN TO ACTIVATE YOUR UNIQUE GIFT

Here's today's Evolutionary Love code:

> You are not just a Unique Self, but you are an Evolutionary Unique Self.

I (Barbara) am aware that in this church we are celebrating the planetary birth of humanity as a co-evolving species. I believe we are the first church to have this as our unique expression.

Today, we are celebrating the birthday of Marc Gafni, who is our partner in activating and celebrating the planetary birth for all humanity. The planetary birth means that each individual within the planetary body is awakening to their own uniqueness and their own expression of genius. **When we resonate the celebration of the birthday of an evolutionary agent, we realize that nature has given birth to him for exactly the time when this is needed for planetary evolution.**

Some people are born exactly as needed. For example, Abraham Lincoln was born for the time of the whole Civil War, or Winston Churchill was born at the time of the Nazis. *Never give in, never, never, never*, he said.

I (Barbara) believe that Marc has been born exactly at the time of the planetary birth of the new humanity and that this was not just an ordinary birth; it was a seminal birth. Let us go within and experience two things: the birth of Marc, birthing this church, birthing his life for the planetary awakening and giving thanks for that, and then let's each of us place our own unique gift into the field with all members of this church to be the first church ever to be overtly celebrating humanity's birth as a co-evolving, co-creative species guided by Evolutionary Love.

This is the new template. This is the new purpose. This is the new code of evolution, and we celebrate Marc as an embodiment, an activator, and a lover of that great potential for humanity.

It coincides with *Yom Kippur* which is the holiest day in the Hebrew calendar. I (Marc) want to talk a little bit about *Yom Kippur* as we talk about our code. I am delighted to celebrate with you my birthday and where would be a better place to celebrate birthdays and our code than in Evolutionary Church? On *Yom Kippur,* we say *Yom Tov*.

We need a Catholic blessing when we do Catholic holidays and Jewish blessings and Indian blessings, and now on *Yom Kippur* it is a little Jewish moment. We say *Yom Tov* and any people who remember *Yom Kippur* or *Rosh Hashanah* will know.

Let's talk about our evolutionary codes. What a delight, what a delight to be here. We are about to celebrate the end of our first year as we convene here in Bethlehem, as we convene the new church, as we respond to the crisis, and as we always say, *crisis precedes the birth.*

We do this by initiating the new vision as they did in the Renaissance like da Vinci and his friends in Florence. We are in Florence now; we are in virtual Florence. We are initiating the new vision, the five keys: a new world story, new vision of identity, new practices, new vision of community, and new map. We are introducing our evolutionary codes, and *May we be inscribed in the Book of Life together as we initiate these evolutionary codes.*

Our first codes were about Unique Self, recognizing:

- You are a Unique Self. You are an irreducible unique expression of the LoveIntelligence and LoveBeauty that is the initiating and animating Eros and energy of All-That-Is.
- Your Unique Self is a combination of your unique quality of intimacy and your unique perspective that never was, is, or will be other than through you.
- Your unique quality of intimacy and your unique perspective fosters your unique gift that is unlike any other, and that unique gift is needed by All-That-Is.
- **You were born to activate your unique gift.** When you don't activate your unique gift, there is a corner of the world that is un-loved, there is a corner of the world that is empty because your unique gift, which is your unique frequency of light, allows you to stand on the abyss of darkness and say *let there be light* in a way that no one that ever was, is, or will be can ever do.
- The world needs your gift.

To know that I fit—survival of the fittest—means, *I know I fit in because I am giving my unique gift.* **My unique gift is that which activates me.** Activating my unique gift is the delight, the passion, the purpose, the poignancy, the poetry, and the prose of my life. It is what makes my life potent, and if I had any other p's I would add them on also, but that is the end of my p's for now. Here we go, our Evolutionary Love code coming at you:

You are not just a Unique Self, but you are an Evolutionary Unique Self.

The code simply says something very simple: evolution doesn't happen out there. It is not a theory out there. Evolution happens as interiors and exteriors all the way up and all the way down. We are, I am evolution! **The evolutionary impulse awakens *in me*.** That means I am not just a Unique Self; I am an Evolutionary Unique Self. Evolution is awakening in me.

Oh my God, that code is going to blow us out of the water, and we bring that code into prayer because *evolution awakening in me* is not merely a *perfect robotic being*, but it is a *being intended by evolution with stories*. With stories that are beautiful and stories that are complex, and some stories we have to let go of and others we have to hold on to.

FORGIVENESS AND YOM KIPPUR: YOU ARE HELD ACCOUNTABLE BECAUSE YOU ARE LOVED

We have *Yom Kippur*, so we can forgive each other because we are all holy and broken *Hallelujahs*. There is a beautiful teaching: if there is one person you hate in the world, you can't be a lover. This is why on the day of a wedding, the day of your wedding is your *Yom Kippur*. The reason you have *Yom Kippur*, the day of forgiveness, on the day of your wedding is because on the day of your wedding, you have to be a lover. **If there is one person in the world you haven't forgiven, you can't love.** To forgive is not—I want to say this so deeply—to forgive doesn't mean you let go of integrity and you let go of justice.

To forgive means you let go of hatred in your heart.

You may hold others accountable. Holding others accountable is essential. Forgiveness doesn't mean we don't hold accountable. Love holds people accountable. God loves us so much that God wants us to be accountable, not in some crazy judgment, but in the dignity of our lives. Our lives are dignified. *Therefore,* they are accountable. You get that? That is a gorgeous idea!

I am accountable because I am loved, and love perceives my dignity.

We let go of hatred in our hearts. We take right action. We take powerful action, but we let go of hatred in our hearts. That is what we do at *Yom Kippur* and here in church. We embrace our holy and our broken *Hallelujah.*

We embrace the child in us that is alive and awake on our birthday, and we wonder, *oh my god, how did I get to be twenty-six? I can't even imagine how this happened! I feel like I am eighteen!*

I embrace the holy and the broken *Hallelujah.* I forgive everyone. I let go of all the hatred in my heart. We all do it together, and we step into *Hallelujah. Hallelujah,* which means *drunken intoxication* and *pristine praise,* and we open up to our prayer now. Welcome beloveds, welcome everyone to the new revolution.

In Evolutionary Church, we are evolving what prayer means, and *we* are evolving. We're participating in the evolution of God.

Nikos Kazantzakis[15] said *we are the saviors of God,* meaning **God lives in us and holds us, and God depends on us; God needs us to evolve.** That is what we are going to talk about here.

We have to evolve prayer. Prayer is not prayer to a Santa Claus god. Prayer is a movement towards the Infinity of Intimacy, the personal face of Cosmos that knows our name and cares radically and deeply about every single detail of our lives.

We pray, and we offer prayer for ourselves. Prayer affirms the dignity of personal need. We offer prayer for every single person in the world, for every single animal in the world, but we don't forget about ourselves.

---

15   Nikos Kazantzakis (1883–1957) was a Greek writer, philosopher, and thinker best known for works like *Zorba the Greek, The Last Temptation of Christ,* and *The Saviors of God: Spiritual Exercises.*

We put our needs, our holy and our broken *Hallelujah* on the altar of Evolutionary Church as we reclaim prayer.

We loosen the fundamentalist grip on prayer. Prayer is not prayer to an ethnocentric homophobic god. Prayer is prayer to the Infinity of Intimacy, the ultimate personal force in the world that lives in us and holds us. Rumi falls into the arms of the Beloved.

It is to the Beloved that we turn, the infinitely powerful, exponentially beyond imagination powerful and intimate divinity, and we say, *I pray!*

Let's pray, friends. Let's pray for each other.

Let's offer our prayers; the prayers rock the heavens. Every prayer opens up another gate. Oh my God!

And we lift these prayers to the sky. As Rumi said, *Let me lift you like a prayer to the sky*!

Let's lift our prayers together with thousands of people in Evolutionary Church to set this new movement in motion.

Let's be excited! Let's bring the good news! Let's forgive each other, my friends, and let's rock it open!

GOD'S INTENTION TO CREATE CO-CREATORS IS EMERGING

I am putting my attention for a moment on God and God's intention. Obviously, it is an intentional universe because it is always more creative, more loving, more aware for billions and billions of years of God's intention.

It could be that right now, in the time of the planetary birth, this multi-billion-year effort of the Divine to create ever more conscious beings is residing in each one of us.

We happen to be born at the time when God's intention to create co-creators is emerging.

He couldn't have created co-creators with Neanderthals. He couldn't have done it even with very early *Homo sapiens*. He is doing it right now at the very edge of devolution because birth is dangerous. **Birth is dangerous!** We are the church founded in the exact moment of God's intention to arise among us evolutionary humans.

I want to place our code in the purpose of God to create co-creators: The first part of the code is, *you are an Evolutionary Unique Self,* the awesome Reality that out of the billions and billions of years of evolution that evolution has shown up uniquely as you to express something that only you can give. If we dwell on that for a moment, it is way beyond the ordinary identity. I remember when I first discovered that I am evolution and felt that I was conscious evolution. I had something to do about it, that is to say *uniquely me.*

People around me said *You must be out of your mind to think you are going to influence evolution.* Evolution felt like this enormous process of creation which could hardly ever be influenced by any individual, but I was experiencing, *I am evolution in person making choices.*

Let's take for each of us now:

We are each an Evolutionary Unique Self, meaning that the interior of us has come from the billions of years of evolution connecting separate parts to make a new whole, a love affair, through allurement and attraction.

We are each an Evolutionary Unique Self filled with this passionate attraction of particles to create more complex beings uniquely waking up as you and me in the Evolutionary Church. You could do a cosmic drama about this moment!

To look at ourselves as Evolutionary Unique Selves requires an evolutionary context. An evolutionary context is an overview of Reality that most people, even those who are very intelligent—dealing with improving health, education, economics, or politics—don't see. They do not place our turn on the spiral in a multi-billion-year tendency of evolution, which is to create higher order through connecting separate parts to make a new whole. They do not see the pattern of evolution in the political chaos that we have. When we look at the current situation of our own uniqueness in an evolutionary context of the breakdown of our political, social, and environmental systems, what this means is so awesome. This is the exact moment for the unique evolutionary individual to show up with the self-confidence, the confidence in that Unique Self coming from the source of creation to be able to affirm: *Yes, I have an evolutionary relationship to life that is uniquely my own, and it is needed by All-That-Is.*

- ◆ It is needed by me to say *Yes.*
- ◆ I am not affirming out of ego.
- ◆ I am affirming out of essence because I know I am an expression of the entire process of creation uniquely as me evolving.

If anybody really feels that, there is almost no word for the glory of each of us. Glory, glory, *Hallelujah*! There is almost no word. *Mine eyes have seen the glory!* I know, and *mine eyes have felt the glory!* My eyes have noticed: *I am the glory.* You see, that is the big one. I am the glory! I am evolution. I am the glory, and not only that. **I am the evolutionary impulse awake and aware.**

I am taking the code said slightly differently here one by one by one. Let's start with this one: I am the evolutionary impulse awake and aware.

I feel that we can feel, in this moment, the impulse in you and me to express and be our full potential selves as the entire impulse of creation becoming aware uniquely. Just let that sink in.

118

I am the entire process of creation becoming aware—uniquely as me—as an impulse to express my full potential as part of the awakening of the entire planet.

See the glorious self-identity that comes to each of us when that becomes a reality. Sometimes I (Barbara) will take a walk in the afternoon here in Colorado and try to breathe into the reality of the individual in the context of me being the billions of years of evolution showing up on this walk. I am the billions of years of evolution taking a walk! I am this little person who is imbued with the glory of the impulse, and that impulse has therefore to affirm the identity of my own glorious self and everybody else's glorious self. Not as an individual egoic self, but as an expression of evolutionary potential self. What happens here is: **The radiance that you are, just completely overwhelms you, especially if you are capable of expressing it with others as we can do in this church.** I feel us doing that, when we love that *Hallelujah* and are expressing that glory through us to everybody and everybody gets it. I am expressing it through me. Each of us is expressing it through who we are.

Then we get to this part of the code: **evolution lives within you.**

Lives! The impulse of evolution is alive with intelligence, creativity, and divine intent. The evolution, the impulse lives within me, within you. There is a phrase I heard from Duane Elgin[16] that I really like, about the evolutionary impulse: *generative erotic impulse.*

> *Generative! It generates life.*
> *Erotic! It is passionately loving.*
> *Eros, passionately loving within me, activating me.*

I am passionately loving when I am that. Everyone, everything, everybody giving the gift freely that was given unto me. You can see the glorious

---

16   Duane Elgin is an internationally recognized author, speaker, and social visionary known for exploring the deeper trends transforming our world, and in particular, for his work on sustainability and www.choosingearth.org.

humans who emerge out of this! I will just complete it with one of my very favorites:

I am evolution having a Barbara-experience.

I am evolution. Every atom, molecule, cell, entity of my being is encoded with this as this unique person, as you, as me, as everybody, as all of us. All of us! If you get an assembly of evolutionary beings having an evolutionary experience uniquely as who they are in the Evolutionary Church of humanity at the time of the planetary birth, can you join with me in seeing the glory?

Our eyes are not used to this much bright glory as who we are. Our eyes have not gotten used to this light. It is brighter than you have ever seen before. I believe that this code is a basis for us to become the glory that we uniquely are.

Let's hear the song, "The Battle Hymn of the Republic," Julia Ward Howe [See Appendix]

Mine eyes have seen the glory. But we are going to turn that sword into a plowshare, and we are going to know that not only *have mine eyes seen the glory of the coming of the Lord*, not only does the Infinity of Intimacy hold us, but the Infinity of Intimacy—and this is the essence of the code—turns to us and says, *Be my partner. Be my partner!* Does everyone get that?

Evolution says be my partner!

To know I am the glory. The glory holds me! I turn to the glory in prayer, and I ask for everything. And at the same time I am the glory! Does everyone get that? Oh my God, I am the glory! Let's see if we can just feel it together for a second. I am evolution. I am the glory. Reality is having a you-experience, a me-experience. Those are the three declarations.

Let's see if we can declare them and feel it:

- I am evolution.
- I am the glory.

- Reality is having a me-experience.

Let's dance in that glory together—now! Can we feel that? I invite everyone just to write *I am the glory*, just *I am the glory*. Just to feel that through. *I am the glory, I am evolution, I am the glory*. Reality is having a me-experience. *I am evolution. I am the glory. I am the glory*, says the whole thing, and we get to shout it out: *I am glorious evolution!* I am the Father, the Son, and the Holy Ghost! *I am the glory. Mine eyes have seen the glory of the coming of the Lord, and the glory holds me, and the glory is me!*

To *feel* that! To *actually feel* that, to *know* that truth, to *drip* that truth, to *pulse* that truth, to let that truth *rock* my world! I am the glory! And when I know I'm the glory, then I know I have to activate my unique gift—what we've been saying above so beautifully.

When I know that I am evolution, I know that there is not one Big Bang, and it doesn't matter whether the Big Bang was precisely the beginning or whether there was an eternity before the Big Bang, but the point is: There is not just one emergence—the Big Bang kept banging.

There is not just one flaring forth:

- **Cosmological evolution** happened. All of what we call inanimate matter evolved, but it is not inanimate. It is alive. Remember *The Sound of Music?*[17] *The hills are alive, ahhh (shriek)!* It is *all* alive!
- Then I go to **biological evolution**—the second Big Bang and cells wake up—and we go all the way up the evolutionary chain from single cells to multi-cells to the neural net, amphibians, up to the neocortex and all the way up the evolutionary chain to more and more love and awareness. We have biological evolution, wow!
- We get to **cultural evolution**, the neocortex. We awaken as

---

17 "Sound of Music" 1959 original Broadway production; the song: "The hills are alive" was referenced in the movie *Moulin Rouge* and others.

human beings, walking on the savannah, and we have cultural evolution. Culture begins, and that is the third Big Bang.

◆ Then, my friends, we get to the fourth Big Bang, and the fourth Big Bang is **I awaken as a Unique Self**. I know that I am irreducibly unique, irreducibly dignified.

◆ Then we explode into the fifth Big Bang in which I realize I am not just a Unique Self. **I am an Evolutionary Unique Self.** I am evolution. Evolution becomes conscious in me.

It is not that evolution wasn't conscious before. It was. Evolution wasn't unconscious when it was making photosynthesis. Evolution wasn't unconscious when it was manifesting the most complex laws of math, but **Conscious Evolution means *evolution becomes conscious in me*. I am evolution. *I become aware* that I am evolution, that I have a gift to give that no one else that ever was, is, or will be can give other than me.** And I realize, oh my god, are you ready? *I am the glory!* That is it. *I am the glory.*

I am the glory, and this is each and everyone's birthday. *Birthday* means this is the day God said, *You are the glory!* That is what a birthday is.

When you hate someone, you know what you do? You say, *Oh my god, you are not the glory*. Does that break your heart, my friends? Can you believe it to say to someone: *you are not the glory*? When I don't love my child and don't shower them with love, I am saying *You are not the glory*. What a tragedy!

When I take my child in my arms with Outrageous Love, I say, *You are the glory*! That is what Outrageous Love means.

When I look at you with Outrageous Love, you are not a person who fulfills my egoic needs.

When I look at you with Outrageous Love, I say, *You are the glory*.

You are the glory. I want to invite us to say not just *I am the glory* but *you are the glory*. Can we say that to each other? Can we look at each other in

Evolutionary Church and say: *you are the glory*? Can we wake up all of Reality in saying that: *you are glory*? How true is that! You are the glory! Can you feel that? **I am the glory, and you are the glory.**

HASIDIC STORY OF MOISHE'S GOOD DEED

I am going to tell you a little story. This is a special story about *I am the glory* and *you are the glory*; it is our code and how you live in this code. It is my (Marc's) birthday, and as it is *Yom Kippur*, I am going to tell you a story that brings together birthdays, *Yom Kippur,* and *you are the glory*.

It is a true story, and it is written in Yiddish at the back of a particular book, a Hasidic book, and it is about a man. In these stories, you know, the man's name is always *Moishe*.

> Moishe lives in a little town in Lublin, and Lublin is where my family is from. I was just there a few years ago, and it is near Majdanek. It is a tragic beautiful place, Lublin, and Moishe, we will call him Morris. Should we call him Morris? Should we Americanize him?
>
> Should we call him Morris or Moishe? What do you think? Anyways, Moishe wants to get a house, and there is this moment where your fortune comes together, and there is this ability to create financial stability. And it is like, oh my God, we can finally kind of find stability.
>
> He hears that there is this little home available for ten thousand rubles. He is very good with his hands, and he knows he can fix it up and sell it for thirty thousand, but he doesn't have nearly enough money to buy it. Ten thousand rubles is a fortune of money. He says to himself, *but this is my moment.* You got that moment: *This is my moment! I'm going to go for it all the way!* This is Moishe's moment.
>
> He goes, and he borrows from all his friends a little money, from this one, from that one. Five rubles, ten rubles, a hundred, two hundred, and he finally gets ten thousand rubles. And he is

going to cross his little step to his little town of Lublin, and he probably sees my great-grandfather along the way. He goes to pay the money for the house.

On the way, he sees this wagon with two children tied to the side of the wagon, and he says: *Oy gevalt, geshrigen*—what's going on here? And the person driving the wagon says, *Well, these two children belong to such and such family, and their family owed my master a debt for the last three years and hasn't paid. So, in accordance with the law, I am taking his children and sending them to the Polish army.*

When you went to the Polish army, you never came back. It was bad. It was a disaster, and he saw these two children ripped from the bosom of their parents. Moishe says, *Oh my god, you are going to take these children and send them to the Polish army?! I mean, how much money do their parents owe your master?*

Can you imagine what the other man said?

He said: *Of course, ten thousand rubles, just ten thousand rubles.*

Well, responded Moishe, *I have ten thousand rubles,* and Moishe takes out the ten thousand rubles, and he gives them to the person driving the wagon. He says: *Just release the kids,* and he brings the kids home to their parents. The parents are ecstatic, and Moishe feels like a million bucks. He is ecstatic—until he walks out of the home.

The children are delivered and Moishe says, *Gevalt! Oy vey!* And this is where *oy vey* was born. *Oy vey!* I just gathered ten thousand rubles from all my friends. I am never going to have the money to pay them back. I am going to be in debt, and my children are going to be taken away. *Gevalt geshrigen*—what was I thinking?! He can't even go home because what is his wife going to say? She is going to kill him. He can't talk to his children.

He goes to the *Beit Midrash* (the study hall), and he says, *Let me at least sit and open a page of Talmud. Maybe I'll lose myself, and I mean, I don't even know what to do. I'll pray, I'll do something.*

He is just completely panic struck, in terror, at a loss, and he goes, and he sits down. Now, listen to what happened, my friends, and now open your hearts. Open your hearts, my friends, for the Holy of Holies.

In walks a stranger who is dressed in a very fine *kaftan*, a very fine outfit and sits next to him, doesn't say anything to him and also opens a page of the Talmud. They sit there together studying in silence for a couple of moments.

Then the stranger says to him: *You look a little worried. Can I help you?*

And you know, sometimes, someone is in an airplane seat next to us, and we spill out the entire story.

So, Moishe tells him everything, and the person sitting next to him with this fine *kaftan* and this dignified look says, *Moishe, thank you for telling me your name and sharing your story, I'm happy to help you. You know, **you did a mitzvah.***

A *mitzvah* means a good deed enjoined by all of Reality. The word *mitzvah* means not just commandment in Hebrew. It means *tzavta;* it means you are *joined*. *Mitzvah* means you are joined with all of Reality, and all of Reality is in you.

There is one thing that is yours to do. That is your *mitzvah*. Wow! See, how beautiful that is! That is evolutionary mysticism.

Mitzvah means *tzavta;* I am joined with all of Reality, and then there is something for me to do.

So, this man sitting next to Moishe says, *You did this mitzvah, this good deed. You know what, I'll buy it from you for ten thousand rubles. I'll give you ten thousand rubles, and you give me the mitzvah and everything is good.*

Moishe says to him, *No, I can't do that. It is my mitzvah. I can't sell you my mitzvah. That was mine to do.*

Well, the man says, *Okay, I understand. You know what, sell me half of the mitzvah. Just half, and I will give you ten thousand rubles.*

Moishe says, *I can't sell you half the mitzvah. I mean, that was my mitzvah. I can't sell you half, and I am sorry. I need ten thousand rubles desperately. My life is going to be wrecked, but I can't sell you half my mitzvah!*

The man says, *Don't worry, just sell me a quarter of the mitzvah, just a quarter of the mitzvah, and I'll give you ten thousand rubles.*

You understand the story.

Moishe said: *No, I can't sell you a quarter of the mitzvah.* Oh my God!

Then the man said to Moishe, *So, Moishe, listen. You refused to sell any of your mitzvah, and my reward to you is—because I am Elijah the prophet and the bodhisattva Elijah—that you are going to have wonderful children.*

You are going to be prosperous your whole life, and you are going to merit to give so much philanthropy and to do so much good that your life will be filled with joy.

And so it was.

YOUR *MITZVAH* IS TO GIVE YOUR UNIQUE GIFT

It's a story about my *mitzvah*, which is my unique gift that I activate, and when I activate it, I never let it go.

That is our code. It is not just me, my narrow Unique Self. It is Evolutionary Unique Self. It is my *mitzvah*. I was intended by all of Reality. From the first nanosecond of the Big Bang, everything conspired to manifest *me*, that unique glory, that will be able to do that unique expression of LoveIntelligence that is me.

My deed is God's need. I am the glory.

To my *mitzvah* I say one thing. To my *mitzvah* I say Yes. Yes! I shout out an evolutionary Yes! Unrelenting positivity. No matter what life throws at me, I am delighted, *I am Yes.* Your deed is God's need, and I shout out and cry out Yes. *Yes, I am the glory. You are the glory.* We shout out *yes* to each other, and a Unique Symphony begins to emerge.

I am going to tell you one last thing: you can't bypass. **I can only shout out *I am the glory* when I embrace my holy *and* my broken *Hallelujah*.** I can only shout out *I am the* glory when I say *I want to know what love is.* I felt heartache and pain; **I don't bypass the heartache and pain. I bring it all in, and then I say Yes.** I say *Yes* only by going through my holy and my broken *Hallelujah.* That is my birthday; that is my celebration. *I want to know what love is!* Let's do our hymn. Let's shout it out: *Love is Outrageous Love! I am the glory!*

I have been imagining that the whole world could experience what we are expressing. **I am imagining a world that knows this, where the divisiveness of our political and social systems simply fades away in the light of this glory, that everyone is uniquely given to this.** I would like to dedicate my life to this being known to the world.

That is my life. I would suggest we each dedicate our unique lives and that Unique Evolutionary Self that each of us is to be able to give this gift personally on a daily basis within ourselves, within our family, with friends and colleagues and through the church. As far as I know, there is no other place yet on Earth doing this. That is amazing. Isn't that true?

There is no other particular place in evolution where this is coming forth. That is true my love, Yes. *Yes,* we are the glory! Not only are we unique selves, but this church is a unique glory because it has the opportunity to reach out globally. There is nothing to stop it, and we can remember some great moments in history:

- We can remember when St. Paul saw the resurrected Christ and realized that he had life everlasting and founded the most incredible church.
- We can remember the origin of democracy, when suddenly people were given the right to vote and be free. Awesome!
- We can remember the beginning of science, when suddenly they understand how the world works. Well, I am putting the evolution of this world view through a loving expression within an Evolutionary Church right up there in that lineage of pioneers, and I happen to feel so grateful that I am part of this.

I am grateful to each one of you, to myself, and all of us. Let's give everything that we possibly can to bring a worldview that can evolve the world through this church. It really is the truth. What we are saying is: *You are the glory; you are evolution.* **To be the glory is to be evolution, and to be anything less than evolution is not to be the glory.**

Reality is having a you-experience right now. You are the glory. I am the glory. We are the glory, and the church is the glory. It's hard to say this that even the church used to feel that way about itself. Yeah, the church is the glory! We say it in a whole different way meaning this particular church, as I am thinking of what the root of the word *church* is: When you say the word *church*, people ask, *Why do we call it a church?* This and that and the other. **We are calling it a church for a good reason: because it has the roots of the evolution of our culture in it.**

Let us give to this church so it can bring forth the word of each of our Unique Selves—of us as beings who are starting the next phase of evolution right now—out into the world.

CHAPTER EIGHT

WORDS ARE MUSIC: WE SPEAK OF EVOLUTIONARY LOVE TO MOVE THIS GENERATION

Episode 50 — October 7, 2017

EVOLUTION WAKES UP TO US CHOOSING

Here is this week's Evolutionary Love Code:

> You are filled with a unique configuration of the LoveIntelligence and LoveBeauty that is the initiating and animating Eros of All-That-Is.

I am an Evolutionary Lover in the resonant field of the Evolutionary Church. I am experiencing the impulse of creation itself when it is emerging, the first Big Bang, the second Big Bang, the third Big Bang, the fourth Big Bang in resonance with everyone in this church and everyone in the world who is awakening from within with the impulse of love.

When we say Evolutionary Love or in other words Outrageous Love, **it is more than human love alone; it is the animation of the whole process of creation in that fourth Big Bang.** We happen to be alive when life on this Earth becomes aware that it is an expression of Evolutionary Love.

We are now able to bring forth and declare the impulse of Evolutionary Love into our divided world—each in our own way—as we join together with each other within this Evolutionary Church and wherever two or more are gathered. **This impulse of evolution—because it is primary, because it was able to go from nothing at all to everything that is—is more forceful, stronger, and greater than any other force on Earth.** For this, I give great thanks.

Oh my God. Oh my Goddess. Oh my Evolutionary Love.

This is an event which is like Bethlehem. This is the great convening. This is the next step. In a moment in which we are feeling hurricanes of every kind, we need to plant the seed. We are planting the seed, and the seed is strong. **We are planting the seed of Evolutionary Church which is rooted in the soil of Evolutionary Love.**

Our previous codes were:

- **You are a Unique Self.** You are an irreducibly unique expression of LoveIntelligence and LoveBeauty that is the initiating and animating energy of All-That-Is. The next Unique Self Code was: your irreducibly unique perspective and your irreducibly unique quality of intimacy fosters— next code—your unique gift.
- **You have a unique gift**. And your unique gift is stunning and gorgeous and can be given only by you. You are the only one that ever is, was, or will ever be who can give that unique gift that is yours to give.
- **Your unique gift is needed by All-That-Is.** There is no one, any place, anywhere that doesn't need that unique code. You are uniquely needed. Barack Obama calls you and says, *oh my God, I need you!* It's not Barack Obama calling; it's Reality. The actual experience is that Reality needs my service. Then, next code, you are not only a Unique Self, but you are an Evolutionary Unique Self.

We are Evolutionary Unique Selves, which is why we formed an Evolutionary Church, which means that I am living in an evolutionary context. **I am living with an evolutionary relationship to life.** It is what I like to call the five Big Bangs. We got to four of them. The Big Bangs mean—and we talk about it together all the time in different language, but it's the same code. It means:

- First Big Bang, cosmological evolution
- Second Big Bang, biological evolution
- Third Big Bang, cultural evolution
- Fourth Big Bang is when we wake up and realize: evolution knew it the whole time. Evolution was always conscious. Evolution was not unconscious when it was doing photosynthesis. There has always been Conscious Evolution, but Conscious Evolution today takes on a new quality
- Fifth Big Bang is when *we* become conscious. It is *not evolution* that is becoming conscious. It is us! But we are part of evolution. When we, as part of evolution, get that evolution is happening in us, not outside of us, evolution wakens part of itself up, and that is us.

We realize that all of a sudden, *we choose*. Evolution has always been choosing. Evolution was not a chance process. It wasn't a random process, but all of a sudden, we choose.

That is stunning! All of a sudden, the future is ours! That is a huge, wild realization, and it is not a metaphor. In Evolutionary Church, we get that this is not a metaphor, not poetry, not a simile, not an epigram. That is from an ontological perspective—meaning the best Reality take we have in the world based on all the interior sciences, and all the evolutionary sciences, systems theory, chaos theory, and complexity theory—the best take, the best answer in the world that we have to the question *Who are you? You are an Evolutionary Unique Self.*

As an Evolutionary Unique Self, we get to our next code:

131

You are filled with a unique configuration of the LoveIntelligence and LoveBeauty that is the initiating and animating Eros of All-That-Is.

That is you! Reality is having a *you-experience*, and Reality is having a wildly good time, and Reality needs you-ness. Reality needs our service. *Om shanti! Hoshana!* Happy *Hallelujah!*

EVOLUTIONARY LOVE IS THE GROUND SWELL OF THE SELF-ORGANIZING UNIVERSE

Here we are as those of us who are here to convene gently, tenderly the next Bethlehem because it is the ground swell of a self-organizing universe, and the universe is right here. We are just laying down the first cornerstones of church. Reality is self-organizing *as* Evolutionary Church.

Thousands of us are here in Evolutionary Church. Our goal is not to grow in order to grow. **Our goal is to grow in order to become a voice that links the planet.** Imagine in a short while when there are seven million people in Evolutionary Church, and those people raise their voices for integrity, and those people raise their voices for justice, and we raise our voices together because those people are us.

We raise our voices for a better tomorrow. We raise our voices for tenderness and for kindness, and we are activists. We are evolutionary activists.

Oh my God, that is the vision!

It's a groundswell—not a top-down but a bottom-up self-organizing Universe—of Evolutionary Lovers who are not all sovereign creators. No, they are all linked together in a Unique Self Symphony in which every person is playing using Evolutionary Love as their instrument, their unique gift that is needed by All-That-Is. That is where we are.

We look at each other, and *we love each other madly.* In Evolutionary Church, we love each other madly, and when we say *we love each other madly*, we don't mean that we are going to sleep together. We don't mean we are going to be romantically involved and get married tomorrow or buy a U-Haul, although, some of you might choose those as your paths—total blessing.

We mean we love each other madly. By this we mean we're Outrageous Lovers. Outrageous Love is just another word for Evolutionary Love. We live in a world of outrageous pain. The only response is Outrageous Love, so we awaken as Outrageous Lovers. **An Evolutionary Lover is not someone who bypasses their story, who bypasses the needs of their life.** An Outrageous Lover knows that all of our needs matter, and our stories matter. We are not doing this thing where we say, *let me bypass my story and become One.* No, I am a unique expression of The One. By being a unique puzzle piece, I complete the One:

- ◆ Our stories matter.
- ◆ Our stories have dignity.
- ◆ Our holy and our broken *Hallelujahs* matter.

All the desperation and all the dignity, all the disaster and all the delight, it all matters because Evolutionary Love understands that the source of everything is the Divine. The Divine is not this abstract god; it is not Santa Claus. The Divine is not just the Infinity of Power that physics attests to. The Divine is also the Infinity of Intimacy that the interior sciences and complexity and chaos theory attest to. God is not just the Infinity of Power. God is the Infinity of Intimacy, and God knows our name. God is the Infinity of Intimacy that knows our name and holds us in every single moment.

WE UNGUARD OUR HEARTS AS EVOLUTIONARY ACTIVISTS

As we hold this moment together, we come before the Divine, and we bring to the Divine all of our life stories. We lay it on the divine altar, and we say, *God, my holy and my broken Hallelujah*. It's all *Hallelujah*, and *Hallelujah* means *hallel*, or pristine divine service. It also means *holelut*, or drunken intoxication. **All of our wrong turns, all of our detours are part of our destination**. We bring in Leonard Cohen, that Jewish man who was keeping the Sabbath, believe it or not, as he toured the world, and wrote the Book of Psalms again for all of us because we need a Jewish man in church, and we need a swami, and we need an imam, and we need a secular humanist.

We unguard our hearts and we stand as Evolutionary Love activists for the healing and transformation of Reality.

We bring our prayer before the Divine, who not just *is* us, who *holds* us, as Rumi says, and we fall into the arms of the beloved, and we offer our holy and our broken *Hallelujah*.

What does it mean to pray? Dearest, dearest friends, so tender, so gentle, so honored to be here with you. What do we pray for? We ask for everything. Prayer affirms the dignity of personal need. When we pray, we ask for ourselves, for my uncle, my brother, my sister. We pray, and we offer up our holy and our broken *Hallelujah*, and we know that every prayer is heard, and that every prayer is honored, and every prayer is dignified because just like you hear my voice in this moment, the Infinity of Intimacy, that is Reality itself, hears every one of our voices. No voice is unheard, and so we offer up our prayer. We pray to the Infinity of Intimacy—the cosmic structure that knows our name, and that yearns for our prayer, and yearns to embrace us in love with a resounding *Yes*—while we pray.

What I am feeling in my heart is the passion of Evolutionary Love. Outrageous Love and the passion of Evolutionary Love.

When I understand that the passion of Evolutionary Love is coming from the entire source of creation—uniquely as me, and when I say *yes* to my passion, when I say *yes* to my passion to create—I am tapping into the genius of the entire evolutionary process in me. I have come to realize that the God within us is this outrageous passion to create more love; if God is love, God says *yes* to the passion to express your love.

The more passionately you're able to feel that you're a unique expression of creativity and joy, that you're a gift to the world, and the more you allow yourself to feel the enormity of that inside of you—then you are able to say *a huge Yes.* I am shouting out *Yes* these days. You know what happens when I do that? The Outrageous Love, that inner Outrageous Love within me, begins to turn on, big time. In the language of Sri Aurobindo, this is the *supra-mental genius of the universe.*

We are experimenting with a new kind of relationship, which we are calling whole mates. **Whole mate is a relationship in which two people who are passionately aroused to express their gift join their genius so that each can express more of that gift.** It is a kind of passionate love, which we call whole mate with whole mate. We go from role mate, which is the regular family love, to soul mate, which is intuitive love between two people. And then being whole mates means to give our greater gift by joining genius. It would be very interesting to ask yourself right now, *do you have in your life, someone whose genius you want to join with?* If so, you are at the threshold of becoming a whole mate, and you might wish to say a big *Yes.*

EVOLUTIONARY PARTNERS SUPPORT SELF-EXPRESSION: A DIALOGUE WITH TIERO AND BRIDGET

I (Barbara) asked my dearest friends, first starting with Bridget, if they would say a word or two. About two weeks ago, they asked me to marry them, and I did. I was so touched by both of them. By the grace of God, they came to visit this morning.

What does it feel like, Bridget, to be an Evolutionary Lover?

Bridget:

> Well, I've been enjoying listening to all of these words, and I can't help but ask myself, what do I do to internalize this language? And so, I drop into the space behind my heart and in my belly—which is the same place that I love to play music from—and I find this space in myself, and I open up my receptors to those who I choose to be joining genius with.

> This has become a daily, constant practice for me to make sure that this space—in the deep parts of my being—are open and ready to receive, to hear and share. So Tiero and I share, whether it's food or music or conversation or hugs and intimacy. It comes from being in that space.

> I think that in that way and from that space, you can choose to be positive all the time. And you can choose to listen to and hear what's really going on for them so that it can be an authentic expression of evolution.

Tiero is a big, tall man. He plays the guitar superbly. And he is one of the great producers of one of the largest music festivals called Arise, and he is Bridget's beloved.

So, Tiero, What do you have to say about the feeling of joining genius?

Tiero says:

> My observation in this time is that there's a fear that holds a lot of people back from really expressing their true selves and really sharing their gifts. Everyone has a unique gift, and fear can hold them back from expressing it. When you find a partner that helps hold that door closed to that fear, so that gift can really be expressed, it helps everyone around them. Evolutionary Love is more than about finding a partner because the partner is evolution itself, and it is the process itself. And that process is our partner.

> Bridget and I have been very blessed to share an experience together that's very divine. It's a wonderful thing for a partnership. I think that evolution itself becomes a partner and can hold aside the fear to allow the self-expression.

So, by being loved by a beloved, it's easier for you to tune in to the Evolutionary Love in you rather than self-criticism.

How does that work when she loves you, that you get to love yourself more?

Tiero:

> That is a very true thing, and it's such a blessing. She gives me permission to express myself more fully. We should all have permission to express ourselves fully.

> Some of us do, and some of us are maybe shy at that at times. But I encourage everyone to remember that evolution is asking us to do that and supports us. And the fear that holds some folks back is not real. It's very easy, or it helps when you have a beloved or someone who reminds you of the glorious being that you are. You don't have to be romantic to remind yourself.

How do you see your music contributing to this? How does music serve this?

Bridget:

> I expressed this yesterday after we played a song at a conference. We talk a lot about exchanging, and we can feel it through conversation when we light each other up through the words we're saying. But what I love about music is that it gives us an opportunity to internalize the experiences that are going on in our mind and therefore integrate the experiences that are going on in our mind. Much like taking a moment to listen to the "Hallelujah" song, where it allows the visceral aspect of our being to wake up to the words and the language and the evolutionary concepts. Then once you feel it in your body, it's more activated. I love music for that quality. I'm dedicated to that visceral quality.

How does music do this?

Tiero:

> My sense of it is a vibrational communication. I think vibration
> plus intention equals change on a vibrational level, and then that
> can be amplified through harmony. When we play together our
> intention is amplified a hundredfold—collaboration between
> just two people can do that. You said earlier groups of two or
> more; that space of collaboration is vital for joining genius.

Yes, the evolutionary impulse inside each of us is unique. It is a vibration.
It is an internal vibration of the uniqueness of that particular impulse that
each of us has. When I have an evolutionary impulse, and I have it together
with someone else who has an evolutionary impulse, it's like music.
Vibrational impulses want to play together. It's a vibrational field. Thank
you!

LOVE THE MOMENT OPEN: EVOLUTION IS WAITING FOR YOU TO SING YOUR SONG

Words matter. We sometimes think that words are words and music is
music. This is not true. Words are music themselves. *dharma* is music.

Words: *abracadabra*. Abracadabra is Aramaic meaning *I create as I speak.*

To understand this, there are words that cover up the silence because there
is no depth. **When you can't hold the silence, the words cover up the
emptiness.** Then we have to go deep inside and find our place in our heart
to get underneath the words.

There is a second kind of *word.*

The second kind of words are **words that well up from the silence**. We call
it, in Hebrew mysticism *milim,* or "words." There is the speaking silence,
dharma; what we are doing together here in an Evolutionary Church is

speaking *words that are dharma*. **By *dharma*, we mean the deepest words that well up from the silence and uncover the music of words.**

Telling a new story is a new musical score. The new story of the universe is the new music of the spheres.

Notice that every generation dances to their music. When I hear 1920s jazz, I am not really that moved, but when I hear music from my own generation, I'm moved. There is a music in every generation, which is the *dharma* of that generation.

Friends, the *dharma* of this generation that's going to generate tomorrow is Evolutionary Love because in this generation, for the first time in history, without this *dharma, there is not going to be a tomorrow.* It's the realization that the source code of Reality is Evolutionary Love and that love is not happening *out there.*

This is the most important sentence: Evolution is not happening *out there.* Evolution is not a process out there. This is the deepest realization. This is everything! We are not doing like a nice little New Age program, like *we'll have a little church.* No!

We are here to evoke and evolve the source code of culture and consciousness.

We are here to change the interior face of the Cosmos, and this is about focusing. To focus really deeply is the *knowing:*

Evolution is not a process out there. It is a process inside, and that process is the Evolutionary Love playing when we breathe.

We know Evolutionary Love is a unique configuration that occurs as me. Reality is having a we-experience. We are here to evolve the source code, and we know that as we are crying *Yes* in this generalized way, we are crying our *unique Yes*: I *am* Evolutionary Love. I *am* evolution.

Evolution is happening inside of me, as me, and through me, and I have a unique gift to give. **To the precise extent that I am not giving that unique gift, I am not writing the poem that only I can write, I am not singing the song that is only mine to sing, there is a corner of the world that is unloved.** Evolutionary Love has not awakened in me, as me, and through me. Evolution is waiting for me!

We sing the song: "I Want To Know What Love Is," which is our second hymn. [See Appendix]. I want to know what love is, and love is Evolutionary Love. That's what it is. Love is Evolutionary Love. Reality waits for me. Reality waits for me to give my gift. Reality waits for me to love the moment open.

> Love the moment open!
> I am evolution. I am Evolutionary Love. *The moment is waiting for me to love the moment open.*
> I am Evolutionary Love, and I am loving the moment open.
> We come together, and we love the moment open.

Let's download that into Reality now, all of us. I am Evolutionary Love, and I'm loving the moment open.

I realize that all of evolution for billions of years intended this moment, and this moment requires **me and me alone** to love that moment open. I can't love the moment open the way anyone else does. If you don't love the moment open, I can't love the moment open, because we are a Unique Self Symphony of Evolutionary Love.

When we came together to join genius in this whole mate emergence, we said, *Wow, we are sharing this impulse; it is so exciting to meet someone else who is holding this impulse. We want to stand for a planetary awakening in love through Unique Self Symphonies. We want to awaken a species in love. I want to know what love is!*

I would like to declare here that we are beginning that now. We are going to pray for everything, and we are asking for everything. In the earliest church, they thought of life everlasting, and people went into the lion's den because they already believed in life everlasting.

I believe in life everlasting. Another way of saying *life everlasting* is *I believe in life ever evolving.* **It is life everlasting to believe in life ever evolving and to believe in yourself as an aspect of that evolution evolving out of love.** I am declaring that to give our gift to this purpose is the highest gift that we can give.

And that this beloved church, that is being grounded in the Reality of love, is a source point for each of us to make the contribution we need because we are going to see to it that it is told worldwide with everyone else who wants to do it.

We are building beyond this moment.
We are building castles in eternity,
through the evolution of love.

We are ready to play a larger game. We are ready to participate in the evolution of love. We are here, like they were in Bethlehem, to usher in a New Age. Oh, my god, Evolutionary Love! Evolutionary Love, the beginning and end of the whole story. Glory. Glory, *Hallelujah.* We are the glory. Everybody, we are *all* the glory. Who else would it be? Let's build a movement from the ground up:

A groundswell of Evolutionary Love
A groundswell of sincerity
A groundswell of delight
A groundswell of devotion together

Let's build this as we stand in this time of hurricanes.

We stand for beauty, for goodness, for truth, for Evolutionary Love.

APPENDIX: SONGS

THE BATTLE HYMN OF THE REPUBLIC—JULIA WARD HOWE[1]

Mine eyes have seen the glory of the coming of the Lord.

He has trampled down the vintage
where the grapes of wrath are stored.

He has loosed the fateful lightning
of his terrible swift sword.

His truth is marching on.

HOW COULD ANYONE—LIBBY RODERICK[2]

How could anyone ever tell you
you were anything less than beautiful?

How could anyone ever tell you
you were less than whole?

How could anyone fail to notice
that your loving is a miracle—
how deeply you're connected to my soul?

1 Julia Ward Howe, "The Battle Hymn of the Republic," 1862.

2 Libby Roderick, "How Could Anyone," on *If You See a Dream* (Turtle Island Records, 1990), CD.

I WANT TO KNOW WHAT LOVE IS—FOREIGNER[3]

I've gotta take a little time,
a little time to think things over.
I better read between the lines,
in case I need it when I'm older.
(Whoa, ooh-ooh, ooh-ooh)

And this mountain, I must climb
feels like the world upon my shoulders,
and through the clouds, I see love shine,
it keeps me warm as life grows colder.

[Pre-Chorus]
In my life, there's been heartache and pain.
I don't know if I can face it again.
Can't stop now, I've travelled so far
to change this lonely life.

[Chorus]
I wanna know what love is.
I want you to show me.
I wanna feel what love is.
I know you can show me.
Oh, oh-oh, oh (ooh)

I'm gonna take a little time,
a little time to look around me.
I've got nowhere left to hide,
it looks like love has finally found me.

[Pre-Chorus]

[Chorus]

[Outro]

(And I wanna feel) I wanna feel what love is

---

3 Foreigner, "I Want To Know What Love Is," recorded November 1984, on *Agent Provocateur*, Atlantic Records, vinyl LP.

(And I know) I know you can show me.
Let's talk about love.
(I wanna know what love is) The love that you feel inside.
(I want you to show me) And I'm feelin' so much love.
(I wanna feel what love is) No, you just cannot hide.
(I know you can show me) Yeah.
I wanna know what love is (Let's talk about love).
I want you to show me, I wanna feel.
(I wanna feel what love is) And I know, and I know.
I know you can show me (Yeah).
(I wanna know what love is) (I wanna know)
(I want you to show me) I wanna know, I wanna know, wanna know.
(I wanna feel what love is) (I wanna feel)
(I know you can show me).

HALLELUJAH—LEONARD COHEN[4]

Now, I've heard there was a secret chord
that David played, and it pleased the Lord.
But you don't really care for music, do you?
It goes like this, the fourth, the fifth,
the minor fall, the major lift.
The baffled king composing Hallelujah.

[Chorus]

Hallelujah, Hallelujah,
Hallelujah, Hallelujah.

Your faith was strong, but you needed proof.
You saw her bathing on the roof.
Her beauty and the moonlight overthrew you.
She tied you to a kitchen chair,
she broke your throne, and she cut your hair,
and from your lips she drew the Hallelujah.

---

4 Leonard Cohen, "Hallelujah", *Various Positions*, Columbia Records, 1984, LP.

[Chorus]

You say I took the name in vain,
I don't even know the name,
but if I did, well, really, what's it to you?
There's a blaze of light in every word,
it doesn't matter which you heard,
the holy or the broken Hallelujah.

[Chorus]

I did my best, it wasn't much.
I couldn't feel, so I tried to touch.
I've told the truth, I didn't come to fool you.
And even though it all went wrong,
I'll stand before the Lord of Song
With nothing on my tongue but Hallelujah.

OM NAMAH SHIVAAYA

Om Namah Shivaaya
Shivaaya namaha,
Shivaaya namah om
Shivaaya namaha, namaha Shivaaya
Shambhu Shankara namah Shivaaya,
Girijaa Shankara namah Shivaaya
Arunaachala Shiva namah Shivaaya

*I bow to the soul of all. I bow to my Self. I don't know who I am,
so I bow to you, Shiva, my own true Self. I bow to my teachers
who loved me with love. Who took care of me when I couldn't
take care of myself. I owe everything to them. How can I repay
them? They have everything in the world. Only my love is mine
to give, but in giving I find that it is their love flowing through
me back to the world...I have nothing. I have everything. I want
nothing. Only let it flow to you, my love... sing!*

INDEX

D

uniqueness, 64, 68, 69, 70, 72, 74, 75, 76, 80, 81, 82, 91, 95, 101, 111, 118, 138

Unique Self, 16, 22, 39, 42, 50, 54, 56, 61, 62, 64, 65, 67, 68, 69, 73, 74, 75, 76, 77, 79, 82, 95, 111, 113, 114, 118, 122, 127, 130, 133, 140

Unique Self Symphony, 22, 39, 40, 50, 62, 77, 91, 92, 133, 140

Universe, 2, 28, 51, 57, 87, 88, 109

V

Varela, Francisco, 87

victimized, 52, 54

visionary, 3, 23, 37, 38, 43, 54, 57, 65, 83, 84, 109, 112, 119, 132

vital, 138

vocation, 49, 57, 86, 88

voice, 40, 132, 134

W

wake, 6, 9, 26, 49, 118, 122, 123, 131, 137

watch, 32, 44

WeSpace, 7

where we are, 26, 82, 133

whole mate, 16, 17, 25, 40, 83, 91, 101, 135, 140

whole, the, 44, 59

who we are, 28, 54, 70, 81, 119, 120

Wilber, Ken, 70

win/lose, 47

worldcentric, 58

world religion, iv

Y

yearning, 70, 83, 100, 101

Yom Kippur, 112, 114, 115, 123

Yom Tov, 112

ABOUT THE AUTHORS

Dr. Marc Gafni is a visionary world philosopher and futurist, one of the leading formulators of world spirituality and religion of our time, and a beloved teacher and public intellectual. He holds his doctorate in philosophy from Oxford University, as well as Orthodox rabbinic ordination. He co-founded the activist think tank, now called the Center for World Philosophy and Religion where he serves as the co-president with Dr. Zachary Stein. He also served with Barbara Marx Hubbard as co-president of the Foundation for Conscious Evolution, which he consented to lead at Barbara's request after her passing.

He is known for his "source code teachings"—including Unique Self theory and the Five Selves, the Amorous Cosmos, a Politics of Evolutionary Love, a Return to Eros, and Digital Intimacy—and has more than twenty books to his name, including the award-winning Your Unique Self, A Return to Eros, and three volumes of Radical Kabbalah.

He teaches on the cutting edge of philosophy in the West, helping to evolve a new "*dharma*" or meta-theory of Integral meaning that is helping to re-shape key pivoting points in global consciousness and culture, with the aim of participating in the articulation of what Dr. Gafni together with Dr. Stein and colleagues are calling CosmoErotic Humanism.

At the core of CosmoErotic Humanism is what Dr. Gafni and Dr. Stein are calling First Principles and First Values, Anthro-Ontology, and a Universal Grammar of Value. This is the ground of a new shared universe story and a new narrative of identity for the new human and the new humanity. This is what they are calling the emergence from Homo sapiens to Homo Amor. This shared story rooted in First Principles and First Values can then serve as the matrix for a global ethos for a global civilization.

Together with Dr. Stein and Ken Wilber, Gafni is writing a series of seminal books under the collective pseudonym of David J. Temple, which intend to evolve the source code of consciousness and culture in response to the meta-crisis. The first of those books is *First Principles and First Values: Forty-Two Propositions on CosmoErotic Humanism, the Meta-Crisis, and the World to Come.*

Barbara Marx Hubbard (born Barbara Marx; December 22, 1929–April 10, 2019) was an American futurist, author, and public speaker. She is credited with the Wheel of Co-Creation and together with Dr. Gafni, the Wheel of Co-Creation 2.0, as well as the concepts of the Synergy Engine and the "birthing" of humanity.

As co-founder and president of the Foundation for Conscious Evolution and the chair, for the last five years of her life, of the Center for World Philosophy and Religion, she posited that humanity was on the threshold of a quantum leap if newly emergent scientific, social, and spiritual capacities were integrated to address global crises.

She was the author of seven books on social and planetary evolution. In conjunction with the Shift Network, she co-produced the worldwide "Birth 2012" multimedia event. She was also the subject of a biography by author Neale Donald Walsch, *The Mother of Invention: The Legacy of Barbara Marx Hubbard.* Deepak Chopra called her "the voice for conscious evolution."

In 1984, she was symbolically nominated for the vice presidency of the United States. She also co-chaired a number of Soviet-American Citizen Summits, introducing a new concept called SYNCON, to foster synergistic convergence with opposing groups. In addition, she co-founded the World Future Society and the Association for Global New Thought.

Volume Five — Partnering With God

LIST OF EPISODES

www.ingramcontent.com/pod-product-compliance
Lightning Source LLC
LaVergne TN
LVHW011156080426
835508LV00007B/436